G. D. H. COLE:
SELECTED WORKS

SOCIALIST ECONOMICS

SOCIALIST ECONOMICS

G. D. H. COLE

Volume 10

LONDON AND NEW YORK

First published 1950
by Routledge

2 Park Square, Milton Park, Abingdon, Oxfordshire OX14 4RN
711 Third Avenue, New York, NY 10017

Routledge is an imprint of the Taylor & Francis Group, an informa business

First issued in paperback 2017

Copyright © 1950 H A Cole

All rights reserved. No part of this book may be reprinted or reproduced or utilised in any form or by any electronic, mechanical, or other means, now known or hereafter invented, including photocopying and recording, or in any information storage or retrieval system, without permission in writing from the publishers.

Notice:
Product or corporate names may be trademarks or registered trademarks, and are used only for identification and explanation without intent to infringe.

British Library Cataloguing in Publication Data
A catalogue record for this book is available from the British Library

ISBN 13: 978-0-415-56651-3 (Set)
ISBN 13: 978-0-415-59842-2 (Volume 10) (hbk)
ISBN 13: 978-1-138-56441-1 (Volume 10) (pbk)

Publisher's Note
The publisher has gone to great lengths to ensure the quality of this reprint but points out that some imperfections in the original copies may be apparent.

Disclaimer
The publisher has made every effort to trace copyright holders and would welcome correspondence from those they have been unable to trace.

SOCIALIST ECONOMICS

by

G. D. H. Cole

Copyright 1950 by G. D. H. Cole

PRINTED IN GREAT BRITAIN BY
SCOTTISH COUNTY PRESS
DALKEITH

CONTENTS

	Page
Preface	7
I. What are Socialist Economics?	10
II. The Socialists and the Keynesians	40
III. The Postulates of Socialist Economics	56
IV. Planning, Employment and Production	80
V. Economic Democracy	106
VI. International Economics	122
VII. Socialist Economic Values	142

PREFACE

THIS short book has been written at the request of the Fabian Society, whose members were felt to need something of the sort as a starting point for the fuller restatement of economic doctrines in accordance with socialist principles of production and distribution. The need was considered to be the greater because of a growing tendency to confuse state economic planning with Socialism, and thus to produce a diluted socialistic doctrine which is little more than Keynesian Liberalism with frills, or again to think of Socialism as concerned almost solely with the distribution of the national income and not with the conditions under which it is produced. I am conscious of having done no more than lay down certain broad socialist principles which call for much fuller elaboration than I have been able to give them in so brief a study ; but I hope my view of the principles will commend itself to my fellow-Socialists, and will induce some socialist economists to work them out much more thoroughly.

The main criticism that I expect to meet, among Socialists as well as from opponents, is that the conception of economics here put forward involves taking into account many factors which either cannot be exactly measured at all, or, to the extent to which they are measurable, cannot be measured in a common scale with other factors, such as are ordinarily taken as the subject-matter of economic calculation. My answer is that, desirable as it is to measure as exactly as possible whatever can be reduced to terms of calculable units, and satisfactory as it may be to weigh as many factors as possible one with another in a common scale, there are nevertheless many factors which are not the less important because they cannot without falsification be treated in this way. The subject-matter of socialist Economics is the good life as affected by the entire process of production and consumption of goods and services which are either naturally scarce or created only by the expenditure of human effort and ingenuity. Its *pluses* are the goods and services made available for consumption *and* the satisfactions derived from the work of producing them : its *minuses* are the damages inflicted on natural beauty and amenity in the course of production, the using up of irreplaceable natural resources or of resources which cost effort to replace, *and* the dissatisfactions arising out of dull or irksome labour, or an excess of labour beyond what makes for greater happiness than idleness—which is the economic name for excess of leisure.

It is nonsense to contend that men cannot weigh such disparate things one against another ; for men continually do just this, both in the private judgments by which they decide between alternative courses of action and in the public judgments which give preference to one social measure over another or distribute a limited public expenditure among competing uses. In very many cases such judgments, public or private, cannot possibly be compared in their results, or in estimates of their likely results, on any quantitative basis. But this does not make it the less necessary to choose between them, or to choose so much of one good thing and so much of another, when there is a limit to the total that can be afforded. Nor is it the less necessary to decide how much ' bad ' we are prepared to put up with in order to get so much ' good ' —or how much ' good ' to sacrifice in order to avoid so much ' bad '—even when we cannot measure the one against the other in exact quantities. We are continually doing these arithmetically impossible sums, both for ourselves and as citizens in favouring or opposing particular social policies ; and it is the business of socialist Economics, which discards the *laissez-faire* assumption that only 'effective demand' is to be counted in settling what is economically worth while, to take due account of all the factors, in accordance with value judgments based on the socialist principle that in the last resort all men have equal rights to the means to happiness, as far as these depend on the use of human effort in production and on the distribution of the products of such effort.

This short book is an attempt to work out in general terms the implications of this utilitarian conception of economic affairs. It can hope to achieve no such 'elegance' of presentation as is open to those who, setting aside value judgments, are content to move solely in an abstract world of purely market values, and to discard everything that cannot be adequately measured on a common price scale. Morals, of which socialist Economics is quintessentially a branch, never has lent itself to tidy quantitative assessment of what a man ought to do, in order to do right ; and morals never will. But I, for one, would much sooner be an untidy social moralist than leave out half the relevant factors in order to achieve a speciously scientific conclusion. Socialism rests essentially on moral principles ; and socialist Economics is the study which concerns itself with the carrying of these principles into such affairs of everyday life as involve the use or misuse both of the material resources of production and of the human beings through whose efforts these resources are applied to the creation, by painful or pleasant means, of things which people would rather have than do without.

G.D.H.C.

Hendon, April, 1949.

CHAPTER I

WHAT ARE SOCIALIST ECONOMICS?

SOCIALIST Economics are not a peculiar kind of Economics devised to bolster up the socialist case : they are simply a commonsense re-statement of economic laws and principles in terms appropriate to the world of to-day and to-morrow. On a great many matters of fundamental economic doctrine there is no difference between Socialists and other people ; for where men of different opinions are studying the same facts in a spirit of honest enquiry there is plenty of room for agreement about them, however wide the differences about the policies that should be adopted in dealing with them may be. Thus, no one in his senses doubts that if the price of an article is increased without an equal rise in the prices of other articles, in most cases the demand for it will tend to fall off—especially if other things can be substituted for it. Again, no one in his senses denies that all production involves some using up of scarce resources, so that what is used in making one thing is not available for making others. This means that human wants can be satisfied only within limits set by the supply of scarce resources that can be employed in meeting them ; that getting some things accordingly involves forgoing others ; and that the purpose of good economic organisation is to ensure that the wants which deserve to be given preference shall be met before those which are less deserving.

Already, however, this second agreed statement begins to show where the divergences come in. For what wants do deserve to be given preference over others ? The Socialist will set out unhesitatingly from the presumption that the most deserving claim on the social product is the provision for every person of a tolerable minimum standard of civilised living, and that claims to receive more than this minimum can be justified only where either the total product yields a surplus beyond what is needed to ensure the minimum for all, or where the concession of more to some than to others is an indispensable means to increasing the total product—that is, an *incentive* to produce. The practical Socialist may indeed be prepared to modify this presumption of unequal *basic* claims in its immediate application to the society in which he lives ; for hardly any Socialist believes that it is practicable to leap directly from a capitalistic to a fully socialist society. But the Socialist will always be trying to apply his principle of fair shares for all to the fullest extent to which he thinks it can be applied to the society with which he is concerned ; and he will always set out to study Economics with this principle firmly in mind as his objective.

This, however, is not the principle on which in any hitherto existing society the priority of claims has actually been settled. It would have staggered an eighteenth-century landowner to be told that *anyone* supposed that every other person had as good a claim as he to enjoy the means to civilised living, and that no claim of his to more than was enjoyed by labourers and other riff-raff could be considered except on the basis of its necessity for increasing total production and thus helping to raise the general standard of life. Even to-day most considerable owners of property and recipients of large incomes believe that they have a claim to be allowed to consume more than other people, not only because they believe they give the community superior service, but also, and in some cases exclusively, because they are ' gentlemen ' or because they claim to enjoy their ' rights of property ' or of superior education or culture irrespective of the service which they render to the community as a whole.

Economics, as a study of the economic aspects of the life of society and of the laws and principles which govern the production and distribution of goods and services which use up scarce resources, inevitably takes its colour from the social environment in which the economist lives. Economics, or rather Political Economy, as the subject used to be named, grew up in an environment in which most educated persons (and probably most uneducated persons too, as far as they had any opinions on the matter) took it for granted that 'rights' to property and income existed apart from claims based on productive or other social service, and that some men had 'rights' which overrode the claims of the unprivileged majority. Moreover, even those who challenged 'rights' based on hereditary or other forms of privilege commonly believed that a man who, within the law, could make a fortune had a right to enjoy it even if other men were being allowed to fall far short of a tolerable standard of living. The very men who attacked hereditary privileges were often, as in the great French Revolution, among the foremost in defending the 'rights of property' based on personal acquisition. The notion of a prior claim, valid for every individual, to a decent standard of civilised living either had not entered their heads at all, or had been rejected out of hand as inconsistent with the whole basis of the society in which they had grown up.

Accordingly, the classical economists were simply taking for granted what was taken for granted by most of their articulate contemporaries when they adopted as an assumption of their studies the inequality of property claims and of earning powers, and tacitly assumed that the State and the law would protect such claims and punish offenders against them. They drew up their economic laws governing the receipt of rent, interest, profits and wages on the assumption that the State would guarantee the 'rights of property,' including the right of a man to dispose freely of his 'property' in his own labour as well as in other things. On these assumptions they proceeded to frame a set of 'laws' governing the operation of economic affairs—laws which for the most part could not have been operative unless the 'rights of property' had been first assumed. They thus devised a 'science' of Political Economy which reflected the social valuations of their time and place ; and in their 'science,' the 'rights of property' were taken as a postulate, whereas the 'rights of men' to a minimum standard of civilised living were not.

It must not, however, be forgotten that the new 'science' of Political Economy was in its day, in certain respects, a notably radical force. The first great school of eighteenth-century economists—the French Physiocrats—writing in the environment of the French court before the Revolution—had accepted without question the right of the landlord to what they called the 'net product' of the land, merely insisting that the taxes for the upkeep of government should be levied upon this product. The English economists who followed Adam Smith, writing in the environment of the Industrial Revolution, were critical of the landlord's claims, because they regarded him as an unproductive levier of tribute which grew continually greater as a result of other men's efforts ; and they also, in the name of freedom of enterprise, set themselves against all claims to income resting on exclusive privileges or monopoly supported by law. The insistence of the English economists that the truly valid title to wealth and income rested on productive ability made classical economics a powerful force against both landlordism and trading monopoly ; but it never occurred to most of its exponents to question the title to earned incomes, however large, or to a return on savings invested in productive enterprise, or the right to transmit property by inheritance and to receive the support of the law for all these things, quite irrespective of the claims of all men, simply as men, to enjoy a reasonable standard of life out of the total product of the collective effort of society. Their ideal was that, as far as possible, rewards should correspond to productive services, and not to human needs ; and they tacitly took it for granted that owning a thing was fully equivalent to performing personally the service which the thing performed, so as to entitle the recognised owner of a mine or a factory to receive as income the value of the 'utility' of such a means of production, even if he himself did not manage as well as own and, in practice, did nothing except draw tribute from the labours of other men. The classical economists, even when they were Radicals in politics, would have nothing to say to any *economic* postulate resting on a belief in the equal 'rights of man.' Drawing their notions from the current practice of the economic world of the Industrial Revolution, they stressed the claims of production against those of landlordism and monopolistic privilege, but were quite unconscious that the private ownership of capital, fully as much as of land or of formal monopoly privilege, was a 'right' dependent on state-recognition and police enforcement, and therefore had in it an element of monopoly-revenue which failed to square with their insistence that rewards should be proportionate to services rendered in production.

The classical economists were able to take this line with an appearance of rationality because they wrote and thought of capital, as distinct from unimproved land, as something created by human effort and 'saved' by abstinence from consumption, instead of being used up in meeting immediate wants or desires. No doubt, much of the new wealth of the Industrial Revolution did arise in this way, and was based on the savings made out of profits by rising capitalists who denied themselves as high a living standard as they could have afforded if they had spent on consumption all they were able to earn. But no student of the period will suggest nowadays that abstinence, in any legitimate sense of the word, was the sole, or even the chief, source of capital. Much of the new capital came, not from the savings of active capitalists, but from rising land-rents and mine-rents, and from the proceeds of old fortunes profitably invested in industrial and commercial development. The classical economists simply took one form of capital accumulation which was prevalent in their day, and which they admired, treated it as the essential type of such accumulation, and rested on it a justification of the return to owners of capital in general as necessary agents in the creation of wealth.

In effect, the classical economists made use of an argument which related to one kind of capital accumulation to justify the return on all forms of capital, however accumulated. All capital applied to industry in a sensible way was capable of yielding an increase in production and was therefore fulfilling a desirable economic function ; and accordingly all such capital was entitled to a return. This return accrued to the owner of the capital in question, whether he had saved it out of his earnings, or had inherited it, or had acquired it in any other way. If it was asked why the return on the capital should accrue to capital-owners who were performing no service beyond the loan of their money or the investment of it with some active *entrepreneur*, the answer usually made was ambiguous. In the forefront was put the active capitalist, who managed his own business and thus performed a direct productive service which was enhanced by his willingness to invest his earnings instead of spending them on personal consumption. Behind this protagonist loomed the inactive capital-owner, who was regarded as performing a similar service of 'abstinence' from consumption in order to apply his capital to industry even if he was not in fact abstaining from any consumption that he desired, but was on the contrary using his returns from the investment to expand his consumption as fast as he wished. Finally, behind the figures of the active capitalist *entrepreneur* and the 'abstinent' capital-owner loomed a great cloud—the risk which both undertook in embarking their capital in production instead of either consuming it or investing it quietly in land or in the public funds. The return on capital had thus three aspects—a return for enterprise, a return for 'abstinence,' and a return for risk-taking; but usually these three aspects were presented, not separately but all mixed up and in such a way as to put in the foreground the active *entrepreneur* who financed his business out of his own savings and thus performed all three services at once.

This was a convenient way of arguing because it obscured the essential differences between the three kinds of service. For in fact only one of the three—that of the active *entrepreneur*—had to be performed by the man himself, whereas the other two were attached to the capital itself, irrespective of its ownership. It was easy enough for the classical economists to show that capital constituted a real cost of production, because production meant employing and using up over time scarce resources which needed to be replaced. But it did not follow from this that the return on capital, any more than the rent of land, should accrue of right to any particular person. It only seemed to follow when one considered the case of the active *entrepreneur* who had himself created, saved and invested the capital which he used in conjunction with his personal labour of control and management. The question of the right to own capital which had not been saved by the owner out of his own personal earnings was either not raised at all, being taken for granted despite the criticism directed at the landlord, or was defended with arguments which would have looked much less convincing had they not been supported by the obviously productive figure of the active, saving, investing *entrepreneur*.

These arguments came down from an older tradition than that of classical economics. John Locke stands somewhere in a long line of writers who have rested the rights of property on the notion that a man, by ' mingling his labour ' with the gifts of nature—e.g. by tilling hitherto untilled soil—makes the things he works on a part of himself, and thus ' fixes his property in them.' This process is generally described as taking place at an unspecified early stage of social development, when there is land for all and to spare, so that a man by cultivating it is not taking away anything that anyone else needs for himself. But the right of property thus acquired is regarded as persisting permanently and as transmissible by inheritance; and it is also further extended (as in Locke) by treating whatever labour is performed by ' servants ' as the labour of their masters, so that all natural limits on the acquisition of property rights by the exercise of labour are removed—a conception which totally alters the character of the doctrine and, as Rousseau for one saw, knocks away its valid foundations.

On the basis of this notion, capital, other than land, was regarded as a stored-up product of labour, which belonged to the person who had caused it to be brought into existence. Land itself was regarded as partly a gift of nature—unimproved land—and partly capital, to the extent to which it had been improved by labour. This definition of capital as ' stored labour ' was clearly inapplicable not only to coal and other raw materials given by nature, but also to capital *values* derived from the operations of social forces, such as the growth of populations, towns, markets, and other factors mainly beyond the capital-owners' control. The classical economists half saw this in the case of land and minerals ; but they entirely failed to see it, or at any rate to take account of it, in connection with other kinds of capital, except in the special case of legally buttressed monopolies, such as the privileged corporations on which they made war in the name of free economic opportunity. It seemed plausible to regard the active *entrepreneur* who applied his savings to the extension of production under his own management and control as entitled to a return which was partly earnings of management and enterprise and partly interest on his personal savings—how much of the one and how much of the other no one could possibly say. They failed to see that it was quite another matter when this argument in favour of the active, capital-providing *entrepreneur* as a necessary agent of economic progress was extended to cover the claims of capitalists who had neither saved a penny out of their personal earnings nor contributed any sort of personal service to the production of useful things.

This extension was, however, habitually made with almost no consciousness of the transition. Therewith, the classical economists habitually assumed that what *some* men were actually doing around them in growing wealthy by enterprise and abstinence could be done by any man, if he would behave as he should ; and on this basis they concluded that the poor were poor by their own fault, and the rich rich by merit. Thus they arrived at a doctrine which, nominally exalting the right of every man to become wealthy by thrift and enterprise, in practice condemned the great majority to the poverty of wages held inexorably at ' subsistence level.'

They did this, not out of sheer inhumanity, but partly at least because they believed that the human race, through too rapid increase of its numbers, was in perpetual danger of outrunning the means of subsistence, and that every rise in real wages threatened to defeat itself by causing more babies to survive and thus adding to the number of competitors in the labour market, so that real wages were bound to be forced down again in the course of the struggle for jobs. This Malthusian dogma, asserted as an absolute finding of economic law, helped them, even when they had decent human instincts, to repress them in the belief that no attempt to raise the labourer's standard of living could in fact do the labourer any good ; and it also enabled them to uphold, without qualms, the claim of the business man to enjoy the full protection of the law in getting as rich as he could by any means that would increase the total product and favour the accumulation of capital. The richer the business men could get, the more would they set aside by saving to increase the community's productive resources ; and such increase was the only way to employ and feed the people and thus to enable population to grow within bounds without an actual fall in the standard of life. Thus the enterprising, saving business man came to be the hero of the classical economists, and in employing more and more workers at subsistence wages he was regarded as a human benefactor, well worthy of his reward.

There was of course a large element of sense in this, in relation to the conditions in which it was said. In face of the immensely high infant death-rate, any rise in real family wages did tend to bring about a rapid rise in population by enabling more infants to survive. Moreover, advancing medical knowledge was of itself leading to a higher rate of survival, and thus calling for more employment and more food. Had it not been possible to open up fresh sources of food supply and to pay for what they yielded by larger exports of manufactures, there would have been in all the developed countries a growing pressure of population on the means of subsistence, such as Malthus feared. The situation did call, as the economists urged, both for emigration to open up new sources of food supply and for very rapid accumulation of capital in order to provide the means of paying for additional imports. The easiest, if not the only, way in the circumstances of promoting this accumulation was to let the owners of capital and the men of business enterprise have their heads with the least possible hindrance from the State or from anyone else ; and, if it could be shown that as a result the poor could not be damaged and would in fact be benefited, as the classical economists thought it could, the conclusion was clear. There should be a legal system of property rights and employment relations that would weight the scales on the side of capitalist enterprise, as against both old forms of hereditary privilege and monopoly and new claims advanced by impracticable idealists such as Robert Owen and the early socialist economists. Such a system, being clearly for the best, could legitimately be taken as a postulate of Political Economy ; and it was so taken, and under its influence economic studies acquired the shape which, in established educational institutions, they have to a great extent kept ever since.

Even when the successors of the classical economists had for the most part discarded the Malthusian argument and come to believe that wages depended rather on labour productivity than on any 'iron law' which held them down to subsistence level, there was not much modification in the other arguments used to uphold the rights of property. The valid concept of the real cost of capital as a factor of production continued to be translated unquestioningly into a claim of the capital-owner to receive a return on his capital. To a remarkable extent, the figure of the active *entrepreneur*, seen as a person engaged in the control and management of his own business, was carried on into the era of large-scale joint stock companies. The use of the word *entrepreneur* became more and more ambiguous. Sometimes it seemed to refer to the owner-manager of a small personal or family enterprise, sometimes to the active financier-directors who controlled large masses of capital that did not belong to them, and employed managers to take charge of actual production under their control, and sometimes to the general body of shareholders who merely invested their money and played no real part (or only an infinitesimal part) in the control of the enterprises in which they held shares. Apart from this dissolution of the concept of the *entrepreneur*, the main change brought about by the discarding of the Malthusian dogma was that the capitalist, instead of being regarded as the residuary legatee of productive enterprise, who took what was left after payment of subsistence wages, came to be treated as more on a par with the wage-earner—as receiving a revenue corresponding to the productivity of his capital in the same way as the wage-earner was paid in accordance with the productivity of his labour. This view of the matter re-established the capitalist's defences when the original case in his favour had lost much of its force. But it remained as true as ever that the factor-cost of capital was being arbitrarily translated into a claim of the capital-owner to receive the equivalent of this cost; and the translation became less plausible as the active, saving, investing *entrepreneur*-manager ceased to be the typical figure of large-scale business enterprise.

Even the older classical attitude, outmoded now, was I repeat, a great advance on what had been believed before. The classical economists did at any rate maintain that rewards ought to correspond to real services, even if they committed the error of identifying the service done by a piece of property—say, a factory—with that done by its owner. They did reject the claim that some men had a prescriptive right to wealth and well-being at other men's expense, irrespective of any service rendered—even if they were in practice by no means thoroughgoing in urging that their teachings on this point should be put into effect. And they did feel, as most writers before

1789 had not felt at all, that it was necessary for them to try to show that the poorer sections of the people would be benefited, and not harmed, by the working of the system they expounded. I am not saying that they did show this, even to the general satisfaction of their contemporaries. Carlyle and Cobbett, as well as the Socialists, fulminated against them, and many humanitarian Tories, such as Shaftesbury, could not stomach their conclusion that nothing could be done, except by higher production (if even by that) to improve the lot of the poor. They had, however, a plausible case for their main thesis—that of the beneficial effect of rapid capital accumulation; and they were led, in pursuance of this thesis and under the influence of Malthus's pessimistic theory of population, to make the capitalist the residuary legatee of the new wealth of machine production, subject only to the sinister rake-off which the landlord, as a 'natural monopolist,' was in a position to secure for himself.

The classical economists' attitude to landlordism brings out very clearly the limitations of their point of view. On the one hand they showed very plainly how with every advance in wealth and population the landlord's rake-off increased without any effort of his own; but on the other hand, in spite of this, they made no direct attack on the landlord's right to receive rent. They attacked only his claim to inflate his rent artificially by the Corn Laws: the rent which accrued to him from ownership, apart from special privilege, they accepted his right to receive, even though it was in no sense the reward for services of his own. They could not, indeed, attack land rent as such without at the same time implicitly attacking all claims to receive income from property unaccompanied by personal service—at any rate, interest on capital in all its forms. But, as no clear line could be drawn between interest on capital and profit derived from the use of capital in conjunction with managerial enterprise, they could not have attacked interest without attacking profits as well, and thus denying the claim of the very factor of production that they admired the most.

The absence of any attempt to distinguish interest clearly from profit was indeed symptomatic of their limited vision. They were of course perfectly well aware of the nature of interest as a return on *borrowed* money and of the conditions governing the rate of return on different kinds of loan—for longer and shorter terms, for greater or lesser risks, and so on. To that extent they had a theory of interest ; but they had therewith a confusion in their minds which led them to extend the notion of interest from that of a return on borrowed money to cover all capital, including capital belonging to an *entrepreneur* and used in his own business. Yet it is one thing to incur a money debt, and quite another to turn money into real productive assets for the purpose of undertaking the risks of production. For, as soon as the money is used in buying things, one ceases to have the money and has the things instead ; and the value of the things is determined not by what they cost in money but by their anticipated capacity to yield a net revenue by their use. The conception of interest, which is essentially that of a return on money, cannot legitimately be applied to a return on the use of real capital assets. These latter yield what is in essence a ' rent,' or ' quasi-rent,' corresponding to their productive quality in relation to market demand. One hundred pounds is just like another hundred pounds ; but one factory set-up is not just like another built at the same money cost. Even if it had been possible—as it was not—to distinguish in the *entrepreneur's* gains how much was due to his personal labour and how much to the quality of his real capital assets, it would still have been entirely misleading to describe the latter element in his gains as ' interest.' The only ' interest ' in the case was that which the *entrepreneur* contracted to pay on money which he *borrowed* for the purposes of his business; and there was no necessary relation between the rate of interest which the *entrepreneur* agreed to pay and the return he derived from the use he made of the borrowed money. The *entrepreneur's* gross receipts, *minus* what he paid out for all his costs, including interest, constituted his profit, which was his remuneration for his toil and trouble, his enterprise, his service in placing his own and his partners' capital in the work of production, and his assumption of the risk he took in borrowing other people's money at a contractual rate of interest. The notion that all capital must somehow be earning an interest corresponding to the interest paid on borrowed money was simply a delusion.

This notion, indeed, was not fully formed in the earlier classical economists. It became explicit only when first J. B. Say and then Nassau Senior began to attempt to disentangle the personal service rendered by the *entrepreneur* from the service rendered by his own and his partners' risk-bearing capital. Then was formulated the notion of a 'rent of ability' accruing to the *entrepreneur* according to the quality of his personal service, as distinct from the imputed 'interest' earned on the capital used in the business. But this distinction could never be given any quantitative basis; for it was impossible to distinguish the earning power of the real capital assets assembled by the *entrepreneur* from his service in assembling them in just that form. The profits of the business were in truth a return on the productive combination including both the real capital assets and the *entrepreneur's* skill and luck in assembling and using them; and no one could say how much value should be attributed to each of the factors thus combined.

The 'capital' and the 'enterprise' being thus intermingled, the classical economists could not have attacked the return on capital without attacking the reward of enterprise as well. Wishing to uphold the *entrepreneur's* claim to a reward corresponding to his service to production, which included his readiness to save and to invest, they had to uphold the claim to a return on capital, and to extend this right to all capital invested in production, whether it arose out of the *entrepreneur's* personal abstinence or not. But they could not go so far without defending in addition the landlord's right to receive rent, as far as it arose out of land improvement and not from what Ricardo called ' the original and indestructible powers of the soil.' This, however, led them even further ; for it was no more possible to distinguish, in the actual rents paid, how much was due to the original and indestructible powers of the soil and how much to improvements than it was to split up the *entrepreneur's* gains into earnings of *entrepreneur* ability and ' interest ' on capital. Accordingly, the classical economists' dislike of land rent petered out into a denunciation of special forms of land monopoly ; and in practice they accepted the landlord's right to reap where he had not sown as decisively as that of the mere capital-owner, though more grudgingly because they saw in the landlord a ' natural monopolist,' whereas they regarded the capital-owner as subject to the discipline of continuous competition with other owners of capital.

Classical Economics, then, idealised the active man of enterprise and the saver, and tended, much beyond what the facts warranted, to identify the two. Such an attitude, whatever tributes were paid to the claims of ordinary men and women to enjoy the means to happiness and well-being, was in practice inconsistent with giving priority to the ordinary man's claims, or recognising his *equal* claim to be considered in the shaping of economic affairs. To be sure, the classical economists did not make the welfare of the capitalist or the man of enterprise their open objective : what they did was to proclaim higher production as the quintessential economic aim, and on this basis to put forward the claims of their heroes as the agents by whose actions this aim would be achieved, provided they were allowed a free field and no favour one against another.

Underlying this kind of economic theory there were certain assumptions which the Political Economists took, usually without question, from the contemporary environment. In the first place they assumed that business men would compete one with another, rather than combine to exploit the consumers—or at any rate that such attempts as business men did make to combine for restrictive purposes could be prevented fairly easily by the State, provided that the State itself was kept free from control by the would-be monopolists. This led most of them to favour an extension of the franchise, at any rate to the main body of the middle classes, who were deemed to be the natural opponents of monopoly. Secondly, they assumed that there would be at all normal times a supply of workers adequate to man the new machines provided out of capitalist savings, and that these workers would be so much in competition for jobs as to be prepared to accept orders and work hard for fear of getting the sack. The hostility of most of the classical economists to Trade Unions rested on the fear that, though they would be unable to flout the ' laws of Political Economy ' by raising wages above the levels dictated by the interaction of supply and demand, they might nevertheless be powerful enough to interfere with the business man's measures for securing hard work and unquestioning obedience to his orders—for example, by concentrated slowing down of the pace of work, and by insistence on traditional regulations and practices governing apprenticeship, piecework, the ' right to a trade,' and other matters of workshop concern. It was on this account that the Trade Unions remained practically outlaws until the 1870's, and continued to meet with much disapproval from the economists long after the law had recognised them as a sequel to the political enfranchisement of the skilled workmen in 1867. It was assumed that, if only Trade Unions could be kept under, the workers would *have* to work hard in order to hold their jobs, and that accordingly there was no need to consult their wishes or enlist their co-operation in promoting industrial efficiency.

Thirdly, it was assumed that, in the natural course of things, whatever men saved out of their incomes instead of spending it on immediate consumption would flow as investment into industry, and would thus increase the quantity and quality of capital equipment and would issue, in due course, in higher output of finished goods and services. Of course, the classical economists were aware that this did not always occur in fact. They knew that there were slumps as well as booms, and that in slumps there was usually a sharp decline in the investment of capital in new productive assets. But, living in the midst of a technical revolution which they saw actually resulting in prodigies of increased production, they looked upon slumps as exceptions which in no way invalidated the general rule of economic progress. In progress in the productive arts they believed absolutely, even when their outlook was in other respects pessimistic; and this belief enabled them to regard as an undoubted enemy of society anyone who in any way obstructed the business men in the application of new productive techniques, and to regard slumps as mere unavoidable interruptions to the continuing process of industrial advance—or even as salutary, when they cleared inferior businesses and obsolescent machinery out of the way by the hard arbitrament of bankruptcy. Thus, the classical economists felt entitled to leave slumps out of their general economic theory, as merely secondary phenomena, and to treat unemployment, not as the outcome of anything amiss with the economic system, but as the penalty of gross inefficiency or laziness or intemperance on the part of its individual victims, or of Trade Union attempts to flout the 'laws of supply and demand,' and therefore as calling for remedy through moral improvement, better technical education, and, not least, measures of deterrence such as were embodied in the new Poor Law of 1834 and in the Acts restricting Trade Union activity.

The complacency with which most of the economic writers of the classical period regarded not only the sheer misery of a large part of the people, but also the evident failure of the greatly increased productivity of industry to bring with it any advance in the well-being of the large contingent of participants in the new techniques, shocked some of their contemporaries and has shocked many of the historians who have studied the records of the time. It is not, however, on second thoughts, surprising. The very notion that the well-being and happiness of ordinary men and women ought to count equally with those of the more exalted was still so novel that its economic implications had not sunk into the minds even of those who accepted it as a political gospel. No one had declared more roundly and unreservedly than Jeremy Bentham that the aim of social action should be 'the greatest happiness of the greatest number'; but even Bentham remained largely blind to the economic aspects of this momentous doctrine. No one had proclaimed more forcibly that, politically, the only way of securing the actual pursuit of this end was to put the power of judgment into the hands of every man, by introducing universal suffrage; but even Bentham thought it necessary for the enfranchised many to keep their hands off any attempt to regulate economic matters by political means. The Benthamites sought to reconcile this apparent contradiction by asserting that the economic equivalent of political democracy was 'free competition,' resting on the assurance to every man of a legal right to choose his job. They never faced the fact that, whereas their ideal of political democracy rested on the principle of ' one man, one vote,' and was thus equalitarian in its foundations, their so-called ' economic liberalism ' rested on a very different and most unequal weighting of men according to their business drive, their efficiency as producers (or as interceptors of other men's product), their possession of property as a starting advantage, their unscrupulousness or ruthlessness, or their sheer luck. ' One man, one vote ' and ' One £, one vote ' are not manifestations of the same principle in different fields : they express opposed principles—the one of basic equality, the other of all-pervading inequality.

The notion of equality, in respect not of human endowments but of human claims to happiness and well-being, was bound to take time to establish itself, even when it had been trenchantly proclaimed by rising authority in both the American and the French Revolution. Where even the revolutionaries who proclaimed it failed to realise its implications, other men could not be expected, save gradually and by a process of historical contention, to see more clearly, especially as there were behind them long centuries of an almost unquestioned contrary tradition. Even the revolutionary leader who declared himself a believer in the ' rights of man,' including an equal right for all to the pursuit of happiness— even the Utilitarian who proclaimed the principle of ' the greatest happiness of the greatest number '—could not truly feel that the very poor, uncultured, ill-equipped men and women whom they saw in great numbers everywhere around them were in very truth entitled to be treated as their equals, and to claim an equal share in the good things of life. They might, if they were given that way, feel that at some time in the future, when these people had been raised to higher levels by better food, better education, and in general better upbringing, the claim to equal treatment would become valid, and they might make this their ideal and devote their efforts to helping to bring it gradually about ; but they could not, in point of cold fact, be expected to behave, either politically or in their personal relations, as if these others were really their equals in most of the affairs of everyday life. Consequently, even if they had some sort of theoretical belief in human equality, they could not easily relate it to their own human environment, especially in economic matters ; whereas it was comparatively simple to affirm, though not to apply in practice, the principle of equality before the law, and even to advocate the principle of ' One man, one vote ' in politics, in the knowledge that its adoption would by no means endow all men with really equal shares in political power.

In effect, the gulf between the educated classes and the poor was still, in the first half of the nineteenth century, too wide, and involved too great differences in standards and habits, for the application of the equalitarian principle in the economic field to be able to capture the imaginations of more than a small minority among the makers of economic theories. A Robert Owen or a Karl Marx could transcend the limitations of the contemporary social situation, and could frame theories which extended the notion of the rights of man from the political to the economic field, so as to put the achievement of a satisfactory standard of living for everyone right in the middle of the picture of social aims. But this was possible only on the basis of a passionate belief in the claims of the common man, whether this belief found expression in Utopian projects of community or in preaching of the class-war of the poor against the rich. It was not possible for men whose vision was centred elsewhere—on technical progress, as distinct from human rights, or on the claims of personal initiative, as distinct from those of sheer human need.

A practical belief in the principle of equality, as applicable in the economic sphere, had for most men to wait upon developments which narrowed the human gulf between the educated classes and the poor, or at all events a sufficient number of them, to undermine the feeling of the educated that they belonged to an essentially different order of beings. This change gradually came about with the increase in the numbers of the intermediate classes, with the rise of standards among the skilled workers, and with the development of popular education, even at a low level. The lines between the 'better' and the 'lower' classes became harder to draw—not, as Marx supposed they would, sharper. It became more difficult to deny that the claims to the means to happiness were pretty much alike for the moderately well-to-do and the not-too-poor; and the actual rise in the living standards of a considerable section of the working class appeared to justify, and to bring much nearer in time, the hope of achieving a similar improvement for all. The doctrine of human equality, not of endowments but of claims resting on basic needs and wants, came to correspond much more to what seemed within the range of practical possibility, and consistent with the preservation of values of which the educated minority had been accustomed to regard itself as the only possible guardian. The fear of *real*, as distinct from nominal, democracy began to subside—not for all the theorisers, but for an increasing number of them. The flaws in the doctrine of economic liberalism, regarded as the equivalent of political democracy in the economic field, began to be appreciated by more and more sincere and disinterested middle-class thinkers. John Stuart Mill is the outstanding representative of this transition in thought.

Of course, it was open to the exponents of the old classical Economics to argue that this change showed how right they had been all along. For, broadly speaking, it was under the institutions which they had advocated, and with the men of enterprise and the savers in control of affairs, that the uplifting of a substantial section of the poorer classes had actually been achieved. Enterprise and investment together, in the hands of a limited class of the forceful and the thrifty, had made such use of the technical opportunities presented to them by the advance of scientific and manipulative knowledge, that total production had increased vastly and a share in its benefits had been transmitted to a considerable part of the people. It was indeed in the nature of things that this should be so ; for the goods which it was possible to produce in ever-growing abundance were largely such as could not find an outlet in satisfying the claims of a small rich class. The disposal of them required an extended market, which could not be found except among the central body of the people : technical progress would have been self-stultifying unless it had increased consumption over a wide field. There had indeed been a prolonged period over which this necessary concomitant of capitalistic development had not made itself at all plain ; and it had been during this period of 'capitalist contradictions' that Karl Marx had formulated his pessimistic forecasts of 'increasing misery.' But soon after the middle of the nineteenth century, thanks largely to the opening up of new sources of cheaply produced foodstuffs which could be procured in exchange for manufactured products, there did occur a notable rise in the living standards of the skilled workers, as well as in the numbers and prosperity of the middle classes.

This filtering down of prosperity seemed to many persons, including most economists, to furnish full justification for the doctrine of economic liberalism, which could now be re-cast in a much more optimistic spirit. Malthus's pessimism seemed to have been disproved by the productivity of the new areas opened to agriculture : the subsistence theory of wages lost its plausibility when its Malthusian basis was knocked away, and in face of the plain fact that real wages *were* rising, at any rate for a large section of the working class. The new theory that wages, and the standards of living generally, depended on productivity, and not on any inexorable 'iron law,' came into fashion, and was used to hold out the hope that presently sufficiency, if not plenty, might come to be within the reach of all men, at any rate in the countries which successfully applied modern productive techniques. Thus the notion of a minimum standard of living, to be guaranteed to all willing workers and to their families, seemed at last to have become reconcilable with the retention of higher standards by a superior minority, and could be advocated without involving the threat of a social revolution that would subvert the entire order of class difference and economic stratification.

In this mood of evolutionary optimism Jevons and Marshall carried through their revision of the economics of the classical school, in correspondence to the change in politics which found expression in the Reform Acts of 1867 and 1884, in the development of representative institutions in Local Government, and in the establishment of a public system of universal elementary education. In this mood Parliament gave legal recognition to Trade Unionism (in 1871 and 1875), and a growing number of employers accepted, however reluctantly, the necessity of bargaining collectively with their employees, or at any rate with the more skilled groups, who, as sharers in the prosperity of the time, were recognised as having a stake in industrial progress. Economists and employers alike adjured these workers to throw away ideas of class-conflict and to put their hopes in co-operating with their masters to make industry more productive for the common benefit. There still remained, however, the great difference that, whereas in politics a basic democratic equality of voting rights was winning wider and wider acceptance, it was still argued that success in industry depended inexorably on the maintenance of inequality and on allowing the man of business and the owner of capital, and not the main body of the workers or the people as a whole, to call the economic tune.

Nevertheless, the effect of the new position of affairs was to open the door to a new kind of Socialism. While the main body of economists continued to argue that the correct course was to do everything possible to increase production, and to wait for the benefits of higher production to filter down further and to spread to the entire people, a growing minority, headed by the Fabians, began to argue that this process was at best much too slow, and that the right next step was to speed it up by collective action in the interests of the 'bottom dog.' The benefits, it was urged, had been going not to those who needed them most, but chiefly to the better-off classes and to the skilled workers ; and it was doubtful whether there even existed any tendency for them to spread to the less skilled workers—much less to what was coming to be known as the 'submerged tenth.' It was well within the power of society, these reformers urged, to come to the help of the really poor and needy, and to establish a tolerable minimum standard of life for all, without any levelling down of those higher up the economic scale—at any rate beyond a taxation of superfluities they could well dispense with. This approach, in the minds of Radicals such as Joseph Chamberlain or of economists such as Thorold Rogers, did not involve any attack on the institutions of capitalistic enterprise or private accumulation of capital. Its principal instruments were envisaged as moderate taxation of the rich and moderate protective legislation extending the principle of state interference which had been applied already in the interests of children and women in a succession of Factory Acts going back as far as 1819.

The Fabians, on the other hand, putting themselves forward as the new interpreters of the doctrine of 'the greatest happiness of the greatest number,' went a great deal farther than this. They did not believe that what was required could be brought about by any mere combination of taxation and protective industrial laws, even aided by the growing power of the working-class voters and of the Trade Unions. They held that the 'national minimum standard of civilised life'—the Webbs' favourite phrase—could not be achieved without a radical transformation of the whole economic order, involving a displacement of capitalistic enterprise from its position of primacy and the substitution of a new order of production planned and controlled by a democratised State in the interests of the whole body of citizens.

This was the new 'collectivist' Socialism of the 1880s, which developed under the influence of a period of capitalist recession following on the rapid advances of the third quarter of the nineteenth century. It differed widely from the older Marxist Socialism which had been a response to the acute sufferings of the workers during the period of the growing pains of the capitalist machine age; for whereas the Marxists had seen the only hope for the workers in a catastrophic overthrow of capitalist society, and had been encouraged in this opinion by the economists' insistence on the inexorable laws of the wages fund and the subsistence theory of wages, the new Socialists were able to take a less pessimistic view. They could point both to the actual improvements in the lot of the more skilled workers that had already occurred to disprove Marx's prophecies and to a revised version of Economic Theory that made working-class standards of living depend on productivity, and accordingly presented no unsurmountable obstacle to further advance, even within the framework of capitalist society.

The neo-classical Economics of Jevons and Marshall did, however, make the practicability of improvement depend on higher production, and did preserve intact the notion that the workers' share in the total product was fixed, if not so rigidly as the earlier economists had supposed, by the 'laws of supply and demand,' with which it would be very dangerous for the State to attempt to interfere, save in quite exceptional cases. This meant in practice that nothing could be done directly to raise the wages of the workers who were lowest down the social scale ; for these workers both had least bargaining power and were least likely to reap the benefits accruing from higher productivity. Accordingly, if the ' bottom dogs ' were to be helped, it was necessary to look elsewhere than to the beneficent effects of advancing production : and the remedy that most readily suggested itself was that the State, without any general interference with the processes of wage-bargaining, should set by law bottom limits below which no employed person should be allowed to fall. This, the new Socialists argued, could be done by a minimum wage law coupled with a law regulating the maximum length of the working week. Moreover, apart from wages, action could be taken, following up what had already been done in the matter of elementary education and in the provision of minimum standards of public health, by extending the scope of the social services to include further benefits, in cash or in kind, in the interests of the very poor. Old Age Pensions, School Meals, maternity and nursing services, a reform of the Poor Laws to provide improved payments in sickness or unemployment—these were among the measures which the Fabians, among others, began to advocate and to work up into carefully considered schemes. Of course, the adoption of any such policies would be bound to require higher taxation ; and their logical implication was that taxation should be looked at in a new way—not merely as a means of meeting the expenses of government and defence, but also as an instrument for re-distributing incomes between the rich and the poor. This new view of taxation (which was really, in relation to the Poor Law, a very old view, dating back to Tudor times) was not, of course, a monopoly of the Socialists : it was plainly stated in Joseph Chamberlain's once-famous ' Unauthorised Radical Programme.' But the Fabians, after Chamberlain's apostasy to the Tories, worked it out much more fully, and linked it more closely to the conception of a ' national minimum standard of civilised life.'

The new Socialists of the Fabian Society and the Independent Labour Party went, however, a long way farther than this advanced programme of social reform. Though they believed that a good beginning could be made without any frontal attack on the capitalist system, they saw limits to what could be achieved by the redistribution through taxation of incomes which were allowed to accrue in the first place to the owners of land and capital. Moreover, they took over the long-standing Socialist demand for the ' Right to Work,' insisting that, if the capitalists could find no use for the services of all the workers, and indeed regarded as indispensable the maintenance of a ' reserve ' of unemployed labour, the State or some other public authority should be obliged to find useful employment for those who were unable to procure work. This demand went right back to the early days of the Socialist movement : it had been expressed by Robert Owen after the Napoleonic Wars, by Louis Blanc in the France of Louis Philippe, by Lassalle in Germany and by the Marxists of the First International, and, more recently, by the Social Democratic Federation in Great Britain during the unemployed troubles of the 1880s. What the Fabians now did was to link this demand to collectivist Socialism by insisting that the State could never effectively guarantee the right to work until it had become itself the owner and controller of the main work-providing industries and services, and had thus put itself in a position to plan for the maintenance of total employment at a level high enough to take the surplus workers off the labour market.

It was further pointed out that, if the policy of redistributive taxation of incomes caused savings to fall off, as the orthodox economists maintained it would, and thus checked the advance of production through investment, the remedy was clear. If the rich no longer saved enough, the State, as the representative of the whole people, would have to take over from them the function of investment, and to provide, out of the taxes, the new capital needed for the maintenance of an adequate pace of economic development. But, as it would never do for the State to hand over the capital it raised from the taxpayers to the control of private profit-seekers, this would mean that the State, or some other public authority, would need to become the responsible owner of the leading industries and to take over their conduct on behalf of the whole people. Thus, the collectivist programme of nationalisation was linked to the policy of the 'national minimum,' and the doctrine of 'evolutionary Socialism' was based on this combination of Socialism and social reform.

This practical programme, which has served ever since as the point of focus for British socialist politics and has made a deep impact on the policies of all other socialist parties animated by Western democratic ideas, involves an approach to Economic Theory entirely different from that of either the old or the new classical schools of economists. This does not mean that there are no points of agreement : on the contrary there are, as we have seen, many. It does, however, mean that the entire point of focus is different, and that the postulates from which the study begins are different too. The orthodox schools of Economics begin by *assuming* the private ownership and control of the means of production, the private appropriation by the owners of the rewards accruing to these factors, and the determination of these rewards by the laws of the so-called 'free market,' in which both goods and services, including the services of men and women in every sort of labour, are sold for what they will fetch. These schools then treat any departures from these postulated norms as exceptions modifying the working of the underlying laws—for example, legal minimum wages, legal regulation of hours, redistributive taxation, public operation or control of industries and services, are all treated as deviations from the fundamental pattern of unregulated private enterprise. As against this, socialist Economics sets out not merely from a different set of postulates, but also from postulates of an essentially different kind. Socialist Economics is not merely an attempt to describe and analyse what happens under certain underlying conditions, but also to discover what ought to happen in the interests of the general well-being of society and of its members. The socialist postulates are not unanalysed facts derived from current capitalist practice, but *norms*—that is, fundamental objectives which the economic factors, as far as they are under men's control, are to be deliberately shaped to further. For Socialists the traditional distinctions between ' Pure ' and ' Applied ' Economics, between ' Economics ' proper and ' Welfare ' Economics, simply do not exist. Of course the socialist economist has to describe and analyse the facts of economic systems in order to prescribe the policies to be followed in dealing with them ; but he does not construct an abstract ' Economic Science ' based on any set of postulates independent of the requirements of human welfare ; nor does he ever regard Economics simply as an academic subject or as a highly intellectual game to be played for the sake of showing how good at it the player can be. Socialist Economics are always severely practical : they are concerned with controlling the economic factors in society in such ways as will further the aims of democracy and the greatest happiness and well-being of the men and women whose lives they affect.

CHAPTER II

THE SOCIALISTS AND THE KEYNESIANS

THE opening chapter of this book was devoted to a criticism of classical economic theories which may appear to some readers to be hardly worth criticising to-day, because they have ceased to be accepted, at any rate in Great Britain, by many economists who are hostile to socialist ideas. I felt, however, that it was indispensable to begin with classical Economics, not only because it was as a critique of the classical doctrines that socialist Economics first developed a distinctive character, but also because the classical conceptions, albeit in modified forms, are still very much alive to-day, above all in the United States, but also over most of Western Europe and in the more reactionary academic circles in Great Britain. The labour theories of value on which Marx built his critique of the early classical economists have, no doubt, been long discarded by their successors (except, curiously, in the handling by some of them of the theory of international trade), and have been replaced by various forms of marginal utility theory, derived from Walras, Jevons, Menger and Marshall. The emphasis in theories of value, except among the Marxists, has long been laid on the demand side, and the rewards accruing to the various factors of production, or to their owners, have been regarded as shares in sale prices determined mainly by the purchasers' willingness to pay. But the shift in value theory from the supply side to the demand side—or at any rate to 'pair of scissors' notions in which much more cutting capacity has been attributed to the demand blade than to the supply blade—has not fundamentally altered the general shape of economic theory—or had not done so until the advent of Keynesian economics during the period between the wars. Even now, the standard text-books are largely pre-Keynesian, and those who stop short at an elementary stage in the subject are apt to be taught in the school of Marshall rather than in the new, more realistic fashion of recent more advanced teaching. Moreover, to an even greater extent the economic thought of non-economists—of business men and bankers and the general run of politicians—is still based on the notions that were spread abroad by the neo-classicists of the Marshallian and Austrian schools.

For this reason, it is still necessary to take account of a type of economics which, even among anti-socialists, is now current only among the more reactionary or out-of-date exponents of the subject. But it is obviously no less necessary to consider the impact of newer ideas, and above all the extraordinary influence exercised by Keynes's *General Theory of Employment, Interest and Money* since its appearance in 1936.

The difference between Keynes and the earlier generations of economists belonging to the classical tradition lies above all in the choice of the central idea round which economic theory is built up. The accepted interpreters of orthodox doctrine right up to Keynes started from the assumption of a natural tendency towards equilibrium at a level that would bring into use every factor of production that was 'worth employing' at all, and treated any lapse from such a condition of 'full employment' as due to some temporary cause or aberration from this normal state of affairs. It was assumed that there was for every factor of production a 'right' price, dependent on its marginal productivity, that would bring the whole of it into use, and that when any factor was not in practice being fully used, the cause must lie either in the fact that its owner was holding out for too high a price, or in some special disturbing force, such as mistaken State intervention or a temporary breakdown of the monetary mechanism of exchange. J. B. Say, in his famous 'market theory,' had explained long ago that every act of production created, under truly competitive conditions, the demand needed to buy the product at a price that would cover the costs of producing it. On this basis the economists constructed a model economic system which was in perfect equilibrium, the incomes paid out to the factors of production just sufficing to clear the market of everything that was produced, at prices which just covered costs at the margin, and gave superior returns to the more efficient factors in proportion to their superior productivity. In this imaginary economic world there was no unemployment, either of human beings or of other factors that could be used in conjunction with human beings. The existence of sub-marginal factors—waste land, obsolete factories and plant, unemployable labour—was regarded as not counting; for such things were not really factors at all. The manifest fact that unemployment did exist, and extended to many factors which could not be thus simply written off as 'unemployable' and therefore economically non-existent, was then explained as a consequence of various 'frictions' in the smooth working of actual economies, which caused them to deviate from the equilibrium model. This model was usually presented in the first instance as perfectly static, with an endlessly repeated round of productive operations and sales which replenished the coffers of the producers. Technical invention, changes in population, and changes in work-habits (e.g. in hours of labour or in efficiency) were treated as disturbing forces, which were sometimes introduced and taken account of in a second, dynamic model of the economic system. Crises and cyclical fluctuations, about the causes of which there was endless argument, were similarly regarded as disturbing forces of a second order, which needed explaining, but only as deviations from what ought to happen in a properly functioning economic system.

What Keynes did was to focus attention on the problem of employment, as the central matter in economic theory. He was by no means the first economist to attempt this; but, partly because of his great ability but even more because of the conditions under which he wrote, he was able to persuade his contemporaries to take seriously a number of doctrines which nearly all the professional economists had previously dismissed as the notions of cranks. I have a lively memory, in my young days, of attending lectures at which the economic ideas of J. A. Hobson were denounced and ridiculed, and of having been regarded by not a few of my own pupils as an utterly unsound economist because I tried to teach them, largely under Hobson's influence, economic conceptions which suddenly became respectable when Keynes so ably restated them in an environment of what appeared to be insoluble long-term unemployment. The queues outside the Employment Exchanges, the desolation of the Distressed Areas, the hunger marches, and the immense expenditure on 'doles' for doing nothing co-operated with Keynes's expositions—which indeed they also inspired—to bring about a revolution in economic theory as an academic subject, and left the anti-Keynesians fighting, even in the United States, what became more and more evidently a losing battle.

The upshot of Keynes's new theory was to make people see that the 'full employment' which the orthodox economists had begun by assuming was not in reality a normal tendency that would assert itself under capitalism in the absence of special disturbing causes, but was, on the contrary, an objective to be aimed at by positive action to bring it about and to maintain it. Keynes showed that, whereas the orthodox economists had been taking for granted that 'equilibrium' would mean full employment, there could in fact be equilibrium *at any level*, from full employment to no employment at all. Supply and demand could balance, not only with all the factors of production in use, but equally with many of them out of use : nor was there any natural tendency, when some of the factors had fallen out of use, for them to be brought back into use in the absence of definite measures designed to secure this effect.

The best-known part of this demonstration was that in which Keynes treated of the problem of saving and investment. Until he wrote, it had been common to assume that every act of saving—that is, of abstention from consuming one's whole income—carried with it an equivalent investment in real capital, and thus took off the market enough goods to offset the costs of production and make it profitable to keep the factors of production in recurrent use. Keynes showed—what now seems obvious—that mere abstention from consuming things can create no demand, and that demand will be created on a sufficient scale only if each act of saving is accompanied by the application of an equal sum of money to the purchase of capital goods—that is, by real investment of a corresponding value. But savers, merely by saving, do not in fact bring about any investment at all. The volume of investment depends on the *entrepreneurs*, private or public, who take up money in shares or loans or by using their own savings in a productive way. If there is for any reason a reduced readiness to apply money to the purchase of capital goods, the total demand for labour will be bound to fall off, unless there is a simultaneous and equivalent increase in spending on consumption. This, however, unless it is artificially induced, is most unlikely to happen : indeed, the decrease in demand for capital goods will cause some of the producers of such goods to lose their incomes, and will thus bring about a fall in consumption as well. When this has happened, a new equilibrium between supply and demand may be established at a lower level, with some of the factors of production out of use; nor will there be any necessary tendency for these factors to be re-employed.

But, if equilibrium could exist at *any* level of employment and production, what became of the beautiful conception of natural forces always making for the best of possible economic worlds, and only thwarted by foolish, even if well meant, interference by Governments, or inflation-loving financiers, or get-rich-quick speculators, or whoever or whatever it was that lurked behind the inconvenient phenomenon of the trade cycle? The entire edifice of *laissez-faire* economic theory collapsed like a house of cards if it had to be admitted that the equilibrium beloved of orthodox economists gave no guarantee of high production or against persistent unemployment. And, when one looked at the facts—the unpleasant facts of the period between the wars—was it not evident that Keynes was in the right? The orthodox economists were, no doubt, still busy explaining that the depression into which the capitalist world had fallen was due to this or that aberration from sound economic behaviour, and that the attempts of Governments to cure the disease by tariffs, work-making, cheap money, and the rest of the expedients they had been driven to were really making the situation a great deal worse. But their lamentations were becoming less and less convincing, the more so because the remedy they seemed most to favour was that of making depression still deeper by deliberate deflation and government 'economy' in order to make things better "in the long run." As Keynes exclaimed impatiently, "in the long run we are all dead."

Keynes, then, constructed a new kind of Economics of which the principal lesson was that it was the State's business to maintain a condition of full employment, instead of trusting to the working of 'economic laws' to bring such a condition about. It was the State's business, Keynes argued, to ensure that there should be enough demand in the market to clear all that could be produced at prices adequate to cover costs, including normal profits. This should be accepted as a definite responsibility of the Government—of course, with the addition that there should not be too much demand either, only just enough to hold things steady *and progressive*, in a condition of dynamic equilibrium deliberately brought about by wise economic planning, not naturally happening when nothing was done to induce it.

Once this idea was accepted, there were plenty of ways of acting on it. Public capital expenditure to fill in the gap left by inadequate private investment, or alternately subsidies to business men designed to induce them to take up capital more freely, or, on a different tack, increased consuming power engendered by tax remissions or, alternatively, by actual subsidies to consumption. Monetary inflation Keynes did not urge ; but he did agree that the banking system ought to stand ready to create enough credit to finance the requirements of full employment. He wanted monetary policy to become the servant of productive development, not an independent and capricious power whose dictates industry had to obey. He treated the rate of interest, not as a sacred thing to which production had to accommodate itself, but as an instrument that could be regulated by public action to help bring about a lightening of the dead hand of unearned income. Therewith, he played ducks and drakes with the time-honoured notion that an annually balanced budget—or indeed a balanced budget at all—was a *sine qua non* of economic rationality. A budget deficit, that is, the State paying out more than it received in taxes—might be the very best way to maintain employment and production in face of a threatened recession in demand. Keynes knocked down the shibboleths of economic orthodoxy, row upon row, with a consummate skill that even his bitterest opponents had to admire. Within a few years he transformed traditional economics from a jeremiad into a practical programme for making the capitalist system work.

No : that is not quite fair. Keynes had no devotion to the capitalist system as such. Indeed, the entire dispute about Capitalism and Socialism seemed to him to be mainly beside the point. His remedies would serve to render workable either Capitalism or Socialism, or indeed any other system that was compatible with the State's acceptance of the responsibility for ensuring full employment. He made this sound easy—if only the manipulators of public economic policy could be persuaded to behave in a reasonably intelligent fashion.

This new Keynesian Economics deeply affected the thought of Socialists as well as of 'progressives' of all sorts who were not Socialists. Keynes made the planning of employment seem so much more important than anything else, at a time when the thoughts of both politicians and economists had become fixed perforce on the disease of unemployment in both its long-term and its cyclical forms. Hitherto, most Socialists had contended that the disease of unemployment was incurable except by socialisation—that is, by the State taking over industry and employing every available person, and at the same time so distributing purchasing power as to ensure that there would be a demand for all that socialised industry could produce. But now it appeared, if Keynes were right, that full employment could be maintained without socialisation, merely by manipulating the correct levers at the centre, in the money and investment markets. There might be a case for socialising this or that industry on other grounds—to prevent monopolistic restriction, or to improve productive efficiency by rationalisation—but not in order to cure unemployment ; for that could be done by other, and much less disturbing, methods.

The only economists who were not deeply affected by

this revolution in traditional economic thought were the Marxists, who, having a complete and distinct economic theory of their own that had diverged from orthodox theory a century ago and thereafter gone its own way, regarded Keynesism as merely the latest dodge to save Capitalism from itself by invoking the State as its ally. Nothing, the Marxists continued to assert, could save Capitalism from recurrent crises, all leading up to the final crisis in the course of which it would be submerged in world revolution. Some Marxists, indeed, went so far as to admit that Keynes's nostrums might prove potent enough to stave off capitalist crisis for some time. Professor Varga, the leading theoretician of the Soviet Union, came near to saying this, and was made to eat his words—though he spat some of them out again in the process.

The Socialist economists who were not full-blooded Marxists were in a different case ; for most of them had no belief in the inevitability of ' Capitalism's Final Crisis.' They had been for a long time past calling on the Government to ease unemployment by ' public works policy '—that is, by providing useful jobs for workers for whom profit-seeking Capitalism appeared to have no use. They had been contending on this issue with the orthodox economists who argued either that the effect of State action to provide work would be an equivalent diminution in private investment [1] or that, even if extra jobs could be provided, the result would be to throw the economic system out of balance and to lead on to an inflationary crisis.[2] Keynes's new doctrines came as a powerful reinforcement of what they had been saying, and as a great relief to their minds, because they were now able to argue for State action with the grain of traditional economic theory, and not against it as heretics and pariahs foolish enough to be taken in by economic ' quacks.'

[1] *e.g.* the " Treasury Memorandum " of 1929.
[2] *e.g.* Professor Hayek's earlier writings.

Above all, the socialist economists in academic jobs, who had to spend their days teaching students the things that were needed for passing examinations, were immensely reassured, and set to work happily to teach the new Keynesian economics, with a sense that a bridge between the classical tradition and Socialism had been successfully built.

Indeed, it is hardly too much to say that most of the non-Marxist socialist economists swallowed Keynes whole, and became his most fervent disciples. As one who did not, I, in my capacity as a teacher, passed from one discomfort to another. The things I had been arguing, largely on a basis laid by J. A. Hobson, at the risk of spoiling my pupils' examination chances, suddenly became part of the new orthodoxy; and I found myself trying to brake the enthusiasm of students who expected far too much from them. For I continued to believe that, great as was the advance made by Keynes in the techniques of economic manipulation, his conclusions were partly vitiated by his habit of reasoning in terms of global demand and supply, or at any rate of 'capital goods' and 'consumers' goods' as global divisions of the total product of industry, instead of breaking up the productive system into much smaller and more differentiated groups of real persons and things.

Thus, when Keynes spoke of maintaining total 'investment' at an adequate level, I began at once to think of the actual forms of this investment—machines of different sorts, specialised buildings, ships, new mine-sinkings, farm equipment, and so on. And when Keynes spoke of 'full employment' I began at once to think of actual men and women, living in particular places and possessing both particular skills, dexterities and aptitudes, and also family attachments and wills to work more or less hard or efficiently. I do not mean that I found other economists ignoring these real factors; but I did find an undue readiness to believe that they were secondary to the main thing—which was to manipulate global demand for investment and consumption goods by making the right budgetary adjustments and accommodating to these the flows of credit out of the banking system, the rates of interest on borrowed money, and the 'public works policy' of the State—which last thus appeared not as a prime mover, but rather as one among a number of budgetary devices for keeping economic activity at a high level. I was sceptical about all this, not as doubting its correctness and usefulness up to a point, but as holding that it left many too many of the real factors in the situation out of account.

For, can the State really, by following the Keynesian prescription, maintain full employment without setting inflationary tendencies to work, unless it is in a position to control, broadly, what is to be produced and when, and what is to be charged for it, and also the broad distribution of purchasing power, as well as its global amount? I do not think it can. I am not suggesting that, in order to achieve *and maintain* full employment without inflation, it is necessary for the State to take charge of the entire economy, to fix all prices, or to regulate the whole distribution of incomes among individuals. But I do believe that, in order to achieve the desired result, the State must be in a position to direct investment into particular branches of production, to control the location of industry in order to bring balanced employment to the workers rather than expect them to migrate in large masses in search of work, and to regulate the course of prices and incomes in such a way as to secure a tolerable correspondence between the flow of consumers' goods and services and the demand for them, and at the same time to keep costs at such a level as to enable exporting industries to hold a satisfactory place in the world market.

But I go further than this. Although it would be

theoretically possible for the State to exercise all these powers by 'controls,' without taking any considerable executive functions into its own hands, I cannot conceive of such an arrangement working in practice, except very ill. Control without executive responsibility or financial accountability for the results of the orders given is an instrument that has its uses, and is indeed indispensable if we are to avoid both an excessive concentration of authority and an undue absence of it ; but it is an instrument that has grave disadvantages—not least the irritation it is bound to cause among those who have to carry out the orders and to bear the brunt of what ensues.

Take the case of investment. The State can, no doubt, in theory, channel private investment into the forms of development it thinks best ; but in practice, if it relies on 'controls,' it has to do this mainly by forbidding types of investment which it thinks less desirable, or actually disapproves. Even if the effect is not that of reducing the total volume of investment—as it may well be—it is unlikely to be very satisfactory in securing the right balance among the permitted types of investment. In order to achieve this, the State must itself become an investor, and therewith an owner of capital assets : not necessarily the sole owner, but investor and owner on a considerable scale, not only in a limited group of 'public service' industries, but over a wide field, covering potentially every major type of capital development. This is apart from the fact—certainly no less important—that 'controls' may be quite ineffective in securing a correct total volume of investment at periods when a stimulus, rather than a deterrent, is called for.

Take again the closely related problem of industrial location. The State, if it tries to secure a right distribution and a right local balance of employment openings merely by control, will be in precisely the same difficulty. In this case it can do something—and is actually doing something—by the development of Industrial Trading Estates and New Towns; but that reinforces my point, for such action involves direct public investment, even if plenty of room is left for private capital to operate within the framework of direct public provision.

Or take price regulation. Here, if anywhere, one would expect the control mechanism to be able to work without direct assumption of responsibility by the State. It is, however, notoriously difficult to fix the right prices except for a narrow range of highly standardised goods, most of which are either crude or semi-manufactured foodstuffs or materials. Control can be most easily extended beyond this field by promoting the production of certain 'utility' lines of standard qualities and specifications; but this method cannot be extended very far without beginning to impinge on justifiable variety of output, and therewith on consumers' choice. Beyond these limits the State cannot easily tell what prices are fair unless it is itself engaged in production and in a position to check the private producers' costs by its own experience, either in publicly owned factories or in establishments in which it has at any rate a part interest in ownership and administration.

Finally, take the case of incomes—for the moment not wages but those paid for managerial, professional, and administrative work. If most industries are privately owned and public employment is confined to a narrow group, there will be a strong tendency for private industry to set the standards of payment for such jobs, and for public employments to have to fall in with the capitalist practice. We have seen this occurring already in the case of the new public boards and corporations.

This matters, not only because it is an essential part of socialist policy to reduce differences of earned, as well as of unearned, income, but also because the example of high earnings in the upper ranges of employment naturally sets up, in any society that is moving towards Socialism, a strong pressure all down the scale for higher incomes, beyond what can be afforded without putting inflationary forces in motion. The spectacle of high top salaries leads to demands for high salaries lower down, and also to demands for high wages, not as a reward for high productivity, but as a claim to higher status and a nearer approach to equality.

It is sometimes argued that this need not happen if a very progressive system of taxation on the higher incomes reduces the real inequality of spending power within reasonable bounds. But this view is psychologically incorrect. Rightly or wrongly, men measure relative status in terms of income before, and not after, direct taxation. It is, moreover, an extraordinary and in the long run indefensible process to begin by distributing much more in earned incomes than the recipients are to be allowed to keep, and then to redress undue inequalities by taking back a higher and higher proportion as the income rises. This is a good enough way of dealing with unearned incomes : its extension to earned incomes is a logical absurdity, save as a purely transitional method.

In effect, then, I am arguing that the Keynesian apparatus for maintaining economic equilibrium at a high level will not work in practice unless the State, through some publicly responsible agency—or rather through many such agencies—owns and conducts a large part of the apparatus of production. This does not mean that it is necessary to nationalise everything—heaven forbid ! It does mean that the ' public sector ' of industry must be large enough to set the tone for the rest, leaving private industry to operate within a framework of public enterprise, rather than the other way around. This ' public sector ' can be itself highly diversified. It can include, besides nationally owned and unified industries and services, state-owned and partly state-owned enterprises in industries still left largely under other forms of ownership. It can include Co-operative Societies, both of consumers and of producers. It can include locally and regionally organised, as well as nationally unified services. It can also have many diverse forms of internal administration, from the Post Office type and the National Board type to various experiments in 'workers' control' and industrial democracy. Public enterprise does not and should not mean uniformity : nor should it mean the elimination of competition except where national unification is clearly necessary on grounds of economic efficiency. But I shall be coming back to this matter, and need not discuss it further here.

The upshot of the argument is that the Keynesian revolution in economic thought is to be welcomed and accepted by Socialists up to a point, but cannot be taken as a substitute for Socialism, or for a socialist economic theory which goes a long way beyond it. Keynesism is after all, in the last analysis, a very elaborate mechanism for *offsetting* rather than curing certain glaring deficiencies in the working of capitalist society. Keynes did not say that he could do away with the inherent instability of Capitalism, with its tendency to engender alternating booms and slumps, with its speculative aberrations, and with its marked preference for monopolistic restriction. He claimed only that he knew how to prevent these tendencies from doing nearly as much harm as they had done in the past. He did not meet even the purely economic case of the Socialists against the capitalist system—much less their whole case, with its large moral and psychological elements.

Accordingly, though Keynesian economics is a great advance on the *laissez-faire*-based economics that preceded it, this advance in no way makes less necessary the formulation of the quite distinct economic theory appropriate to a socialist society. Socialist economists can build on Keynes to a quite considerable extent; and to a still greater extent they can use Keynes as a stick for beating more reactionary economists over the head. But Keynes was no Socialist; he had no deep-seated faith in democracy to drive him on to formulate an economic theory that would meet the needs of a society committed to working out the implications of the democratic attitude in every aspect of social life, including the economic.

CHAPTER III

THE POSTULATES OF SOCIALIST ECONOMICS

I shall attempt in this chapter a brief catalogue of the main postulates which lie at the foundation of socialist economic thought.

> 1. The purpose of economic activity is the satisfaction of human wants under conditions that will not involve more disutility in the rendering of human services than is compensated for by the utility derived from them.

Some services give pleasure to the renderer, and therefore involve no disutility. But there is a point beyond which even pleasurable productive activities become irksome; and most forms of work, regularly pursued, involve some disutility, the degree of which varies with the conditions under which the work is done, the sense of worthwhileness in the mind of the doer, and the opportunity for the exercise of skill and display of prowess which the work affords. The point at which the disutility exceeds the utility created by the work depends also on the opportunities open to the worker for the enjoyment of leisure and on his capacity to take advantage of them. Pleasurable activities which do not contribute to the satisfaction of human wants fall outside the economic field; but it may be desirable to make provision for them in certain cases on an economic basis where they cannot be easily distinguished from similar activities which do contribute to the satisfaction of human wants—e.g. in the case of artists. In general, however, the worthwhileness of human activities must be estimated in relation to their capacity to satisfy wants, measured against the using up of effort and of other scarce resources involved in them, and against the irksomeness of the effort.

2. The first principle to be observed in according priority to some wants over others is that, subject to the qualifications stated in later propositions, every human being has equal rights. Accordingly, the basic needs common to all men should receive first priority, together with those special needs which, differing from person to person or from group to group, are indispensable to the ensuring of a national (or worldwide) minimum standard of living.

By 'special needs' are meant, e.g. the special requirements of expectant and nursing mothers, of infants and children, of old people, of sufferers from disabilities needing special treatment, and of persons whose occupational services involve them in special expenses for such things as clothing, travel, or diet. The principle of equal rights here laid down is the economic correlative of the principle proclaimed in the *Declaration of the Rights of Man* that ' Men are born, and always continue, free and equal in respect of their rights. Civil distinctions, therefore, can be founded only on public utility.' This principle is a fundamental postulate of economic, as much as of political democracy. It is, of course, consistent with recognising that the wants of children differ from those of adults, and those of old people from those of younger people in active employment. It points not to a mechanical equality of all men, but to a recognition that deviations from equality require in all cases particular justification on grounds either of need or of social utility. The acceptance of the principle does not mean that it can be at once or everywhere fully applied. The degree to which it can be applied, either within a particular society or on a wider international basis, has to be decided on grounds of practicability. It may be impracticable to apply a common minimum standard to all the peoples of the earth when it has become fully practicable to apply such a standard to all the members of a particular society. But it remains the objective to apply a common standard, subject to regional differences of need, over the widest possible area and, as speedily as possible, over all the earth.

3. Men, as consumers, stand in need both of a sufficiency of goods and services to ensure physical well-being and mental satisfaction and of sufficient leisure for the enjoyment of these things.

It is, of course, impossible to define what constitutes a sufficiency, either of goods and services or of leisure. This depends not only on changing standards dependent in turn mainly on productivity, but also on conditions of living, cultural as well as climatic, and on the relative valuations put on goods and services on the one hand, and leisure on the other, among the bodies of persons concerned. The tendency of modern society has been to multiply wants, partly because of the growing complexity of living conditions, but also partly because it has paid profit-seeking *entrepreneurs* to encourage mass-consumption of their wares. A less unequal society will be better able to decide for itself what it does really want enough to make it worth while to forgo the loss of leisure involved in producing it. In this matter there is at present a vicious circle. It must not, however, be forgotten that the use of leisure commonly involves the use of goods and services too. The more leisure men have, the higher are their demands for goods and services. They cannot, however, have things both ways. In a democratically organised community, the demand for goods and services will be directly competitive with the demand for leisure, and the adjustment will have to be made (*a*) by setting certain limits to the hours of labour a man can be compelled to perform, and (*b*) by allowing the individual to choose within these limits where to draw the line, subject to the requirements of industrial production for certain minima of continuous attendance and activity in order to avoid dislocation of the productive unit. It may also be held that society has a right to exact from every fit person who is not specifically exempted on account of other duties a minimum of productive service in return for the protection and security which the society affords. This right, however, should be exercised only to the least extent that is found compatible with the society's general preference for more goods and services over more leisure. In other words, the compulsion to labour should be applied only where social obligations are being manifestly and flagrantly evaded.

4. Men, in their capacity as producers, need both good working conditions and a sense of worthwhileness in the work they are called upon to do, and also a status of freedom and self-government in their productive relations, and an opportunity to display prowess and initiative to the fullest extent of their capacities, consistently with the necessity of high production to meet the consumers' needs.

It has been traditional in Economic Theory to treat the achievement of the highest possible production as the sole end of economic activity, and to measure the quantity of production solely by reference to the demands of the market, irrespective of the lack of correspondence between the distribution of purchasing power and that of human needs. For socialist Economics it is not enough simply to insist that a criterion of need shall be substituted for that of an unregulated market demand: it is also necessary to take into account the conditions of production. It has been already emphasised that higher production is to be desired not absolutely, but only up to the point at which the disutility involved in it exceeds the utility of the product. This disutility depends, not only on the duration and intensity of labour, but also on the physical and human conditions under which the labour is performed. The criterion of worthwhileness will be satisfied where the standard of priorities is settled in accordance with needs rather than with unregulated demands ; but it is also necessary to ensure good conditions of work, conducive to health and happiness, and to recognise the human claim of the worker to be treated as a social equal even where the discipline of production requires that he shall work under orders. This involves, not merely that the workers shall be ' consulted ' by those in authority, both in the workshops and at all higher levels of industrial management, but also that the workshop and the whole structure of industry shall be democratised, at least to the same extent as politics are democratised, or intended to be so in a socialist society. No one supposes that political democracy involves either decision of all matters by mass meetings or the direct election of all administrative officers or the exercise of equal influence by all the citizens, even if all have equal voting rights. Similarly, economic democracy does not involve any of these things ; but it does involve that there shall be, in industry, both representative institutions resting on the democratic principle of free discussion and majority decision, and an opportunity for every worker to exercise civic rights corresponding to those of the elector in political affairs. The application of these rights in industry is limited, however, by the overriding principle that it is for the entire community of consumers, and not for particular groups of producers, to settle what is to be given priority in allocating resources to the various forms of production, and how incomes are to be distributed in accordance with the principles of social utility. The producer's right is to the assurance that his efforts will be neither wasted on relatively useless products nor rendered more irksome than the necessities of the productive system require.

5. Men, both as producers and as consumers, need security, which has two main aspects—security of real income, and security of employment. Neither of these claims can be absolute; for the real income that can be afforded may vary with the ability of a society to meet the wants of its members either directly out of its own production or by exchange with other societies, and the claim to security of employment may conflict with the need to alter the allocation of man-power to the different kinds of production and service. Nevertheless, it is a postulate of socialist Economics that real incomes shall not be allowed to fluctuate (as distinct from a steady increase) more than the circumstances of the whole society render unavoidable, and also that men shall not be forced to change their jobs against their will, so as to forfeit their acquired skill or dexterity, save for demonstrable reasons of social need.

Security here of course includes security of income during sickness or incapacity and reinstatement in acceptable employment when the incapacity ends. It includes security of income for those past work and the proportioning of income, up to a reasonable minimum standard, to family needs. Where social requirements involve change of occupation, it involves due facilities for training in alternative skills or dexterities; and it also involves that, as far as society can so contrive, no child shall be sent out into the world unequipped with the means of making the best of its natural faculties in useful service.

Social security further implies the provision for all of a reasonable minimum of cultural education and training in the arts of living, and of health services, both personal and environmental, adequate housing with reasonable security of tenure, and advice and assistance in understanding and claiming the rights recognised in the social code.

Although it is desirable wherever possible to avoid compelling skilled workers to change their jobs in such a way as to forfeit their acquired skill, it is evident that no guarantee can be given that such shifts will not be needed in face of changes in the structure of demand, either at home or in export markets. Social security cannot carry with it any absolute right to a particular kind of job. It can, however, and should, include an assurance both that workers will not be shifted unnecessarily and that, where they must be shifted, full opportunity will be given them to acquire an alternative skill. Similar conditions apply to enforced movement to a new district. Wherever possible, the work should be taken to the workers. Where the worker has to migrate in the national interest, the State should meet the costs of migration and of resettlement in the new home.

6. Since, within the limits set by the demand for leisure and the requirement of good working conditions, the highest possible production of worthwhile products in accordance with the priority of wants is evidently to be desired, it follows that (*a*) no one able to work should be idle as long as any wants remain unmet, and (*b*) that consumers should be left as free as possible, individually and by households, to decide what they do want as their share of the limited total supply of goods and services available for consumption.

These principles should be subject only to the following limitations :—(*a*) that work must be held to include the satisfaction of immaterial as well as of material wants, and to extend to unpaid as well as to paid services (e.g. those of housewives and mothers), and (*b*) that the society may collectively insist on certain minima of need, irrespective of individual desires, for such things as education, sanitation, defence, cultural services, town and country planning and other amenities, and the requirements of good neighbourliness and human brotherhood in extending help to other peoples.

This principle involves that the maintenance of 'full employment' will be a recognised obligation of the public authority, but that, in the planning of productive activity, the guiding consideration, after the indispensable social services have been assured and other collective needs adequately met, will be what the consumers actually do want, and not what the Government or the planners think they ought to want. This does not exclude measures for the discouragement, or even the prohibition, of certain kinds of consumption deemed to be positively noxious or socially dangerous if carried beyond a certain point—e.g. prohibition of dangerous drugs, taxation of alcoholic liquors, or of gambling, or limitation of certain imports owing to difficulties arising out of the balance of payments. There is, however, a strong presumption against either refusing to give people what they want except for good reasons which command the assent of a majority, or deliberately manipulating prices, save under the same conditions, in order to influence demand.

7. No community can afford to consume all that it produces. Provision must be made both for the replacement of worn-out or obsolete capital equipment, including houses and other buildings, and for the expansion of output to meet the needs either of a rising population or of an improving standard of life, or of both. Accordingly, a part of current production must be set aside for use in future production or for consumption over a long period.

There is no way of determining in principle how much a society ought to set aside for these purposes ; for, subject to a minimum provision dependent on the circumstances and prospects of the society, the choice can be made at will between a higher and a lower rate of accumulation. What is clear is that this choice ought not to be left to the chance of individuals' willingness to spend less than their incomes : it ought to be made socially and democratically, by the representatives of the whole society, at any rate to the extent of determining on a broad allocation of resources between the competing claims of consumption and investment.

The essential point here is that, whatever may be the methods used in assigning resources to the making good of depreciation and obsolescence and to the provision for new investment, the total sums to be set aside for these purposes out of current production must be settled by deliberate planning and not left to chance. Even if there is no economically ' right ' level for investment as against current consumption, irrational fluctuations in the level of investment, caused by varying degrees of expectation of profit from it, upset the economy, both by affecting the total demand for goods and services and by altering the relative demand for goods of different kinds, in such a way as to induce either unemployment or over-employment in the industries which produce capital goods. It is an essential for sound economic development that the pace of investment shall be regulated—not of course fixed, but adjusted from time to time on rational grounds.

It is quite a different question whether the State should itself undertake the bulk of new investment, or leave it to be done by private persons. If the greater part of industry has been socialised, it follows as a matter of course that a large part of investment will be made under public auspices ; but it remains open to the State and its economic agencies either to borrow what is needed from private investors or to supply it out of public funds. If the State itself supplies the capital, without borrowing from its citizens, it will need either to raise the requisite sums by taxation or to levy them directly upon industry as a 'development charge,' with the effect of reducing the sums available for payment to those engaged in industry to the amounts that are needed for the purchase of the supply of consumers' goods and services available after provision for new capital and replacements has been made. Whereas in capitalist societies the normal practice is to pay out in wages, salaries, rent, interest and profits more than enough to buy all the available supplies of consumers' goods and services, in the expectation that a part of the incomes thus paid out will be taxed away and a further part saved, in a socialist society the tendency will be to extend the practice of building up reserves out of current takings to cover the entire amount to be assigned to investment, and to distribute as incomes only the residue. These reserved sums will belong to the public, and will be available for investment either in the industries from which they have been derived, or in other industries, according to the estimated needs for investment in the various branches of the economy.

8. In the distribution of incomes, the first principle should be to provide a minimum living income for every person, subject only to the acceptance of the social obligation to serve the community in return. The second principle should be to provide adequate, but not more than adequate, incentives to effort, including the effort needed to acquire skill or qualifications for higher posts. The third principle should be to consider special claims. These three principles are stated in order of importance ;

C

but they are bound in practice to be considered together. The first principle does not take unlimited precedence over the others, or the second over the third. In weighing the relative claims of the three, the state of opinion in a society on the question of equality and inequality of incomes is bound to be taken into account.

To allow *unlimited* priority to the first principle would involve wiping out the others altogether; for no society has yet reached the point at which it could assign a satisfactory living income to all its members, and still have anything over for meeting other claims. The level of minimum income a society can afford depends on its total productivity; but this is affected by the skill and effort of its working force, which in turn are influenced by the incentives offered to them. Money incentives, both to choose one occupation rather than another and to produce more or better, have therefore to be offered, up to the point at which the additional output yielded by them is regarded as not enough to compensate for their effects in creating economic inequality. The point at which this is deemed to occur will depend on the society's comparative valuations of a nearer approach to equality and a larger and better balanced supply of goods and services. It will also be affected by the degree of inequality existing in the society as a result of the recognition of special claims. Such claims arise primarily in occupations in which there is no possibility of relating the remuneration of services to the economic value produced—e.g. school teaching, health services, public services of many kinds. The remuneration of persons in these and in many other occupations is bound to be arbitrary, unless it is based exclusively on offering whatever wage or salary will attract a sufficient supply of qualified persons; and such a standard is also really arbitrary, because the supply of qualified persons depends on the measures adopted, mainly by the State or with state aid, for training them. Accordingly, the remuneration accorded in such cases depends in practice on the standards traditional in the occupations concerned, subject to such modifications as may be deliberately introduced. These standards are derived from a past in which large inequalities of income based on property rights were in being; and every step taken in a society moving towards Socialism to reduce or eliminate property claims will react on the incomes allowed to privileged occupations manned largely by 'gentlemen.' It will thus become possible to diminish inequalities of remuneration based on traditional class-structures, and to reduce many special claims to the level needed for the offer of adequate incentives. This in turn will react on the occupations in which the output cannot be measured, or the offer of incentives is inappropriate; and in these ways it will become practicable to diminish occupational inequalities of income all round.

It will, however, remain necessary to use wage and salary differences to some extent as instruments for securing a satisfactory distribution of labour among the various occupations, though it is preferable to achieve this as far as possible by other methods, such as the grant of specially favourable working conditions, longer holidays, etc., in occupations for which it is found difficult to recruit an adequate working force.

It will also remain necessary to fix arbitrarily the incomes (pensions) to be allowed to the various classes of retired or disabled persons, as well as to decide the basis on which children's allowances are to be assessed.

There is at present in all advanced communities a sentiment in favour of inequality, as well as a sentiment in favour of a national minimum. This may always continue to be the case; for even if the sentiment against **privilege** becomes general, the sentiment in favour of unequal rewards for **unequal** services may remain. In that case, the desire of some Socialists—e.g. Bernard Shaw—to advance towards complete equality of incomes may never be realised ; for such equality would be practicable only if it were generally felt to be fair, and it could hardly be so except in a society wealthy enough to set its national minimum at a level high enough to cover all reasonable wants.

It should, however, be appreciated that, the smaller the gap between higher and lower incomes becomes, the smaller become the monetary incentives required to elicit special effort. Accordingly, a society advancing towards Socialism will tend to devote an increasing proportion of spendable income to the payment of a rising national minimum, and to distribute a falling proportion in accordance with the second and third principles.

9. In accordance with the foregoing principles, the distribution of incomes is a matter for collective determination, and not for the higgling of the market. This does not mean that every individual's income will be fixed by authority, but that the general lines of distribution will be planned in relation to the total sum available for spending, and that it will not be possible for any important category of incomes to be varied by bargaining without the assent of some recognised income-planning body closely attached to the general planning machinery of the society.

This implies what is commonly called a ' national wage policy,' involving a co-ordination of wage-claims such as exists in part under the Australian Court system of wage-determination. But the principle is applicable not only to wages, but to all the main forms of income, including salaries, professional fees, rent and interest. It also points to the need for a parallel regulation of profit-distributions, where production for profit still exists. Thus, in Great

Britain to-day, the attempt to hold wage-increases in check goes hand in hand with the attempt to ensure limitation of dividends to company shareholders.

Where piecework and similar incentives are offered, the State need not attempt to regulate the income accruing to the individual, but must be in a position to regulate the total available to each industry or group for making such payments.

Naturally, the sums payable as incomes are related to the prices charged for goods and services; and the two must be fixed at such relative levels as will just clear the market of available supplies. The 'amount' of money put into circulation by banks and Treasuries should be just enough to enable all the spendable income to buy at current prices all the available goods and services. It is here assumed that money needed for intermediate purchases and for capital transactions will be separately regulated [1].

10. Just as each society needs to plan its own essential production in accordance with its conception of relative priorities of wants, so the economic intercourse between different societies needs to rest on a basis of concerted planning. The welfare of all peoples will be best served if each people to some extent specialises on producing those things which it is in the best position to produce and exchanges its surpluses for those of other peoples. These exchanges need to be planned in such a way that, on balance, each people gives as good as it gets, not necessarily by balancing its exchanges of goods and services with each other people—that is, bilaterally—but so that, where one gets more from another than it gives, the balance is made good by giving more than it gets from other sources, from

---

[1] See my *Fifty Propositions about Money and Production*. published as a pamphlet in 1936 and now reprinted in my *Money: Its Present and Future*. (Cassell, Third Edition, 1947.)

which in turn the 'creditor' country can draw compensating supplies—that is, under a multilateral system. This differs from the classical theory of Free Trade (which few modern economists defend in its extreme form) in that the exchanges, instead of being left to depend on the innumerable transactions of individual firms, are planned by international discussion, in order to enable each country to plan its national output with assured markets for its surpluses in view, and with foreknowledge of the imports which it can expect to receive, and to be able to pay for, from other countries.

The flaw in the Free Trade theory is that it makes impossible the advance planning either of home production or of external trade. It leaves production and investment at the mercy of price-changes which may upset all economic calculations. Under Free Trade the farmer cannot tell what to grow or the industrialist what to produce for long enough ahead to make intelligent planning or investment impossible. The Free Trade theory rests on the valid principle that the world's wealth can be maximised, that is, most goods produced with least effort, on a basis of geographical specialisation wherever certain areas possess manifest advantages, natural or acquired, for particular kinds of production. This raises the point that this specialisation can best be brought about and can be made most fruitful by deliberately arranging for it instead of merely waiting for it to happen.

At one time, nearly all capitalist economists were Free Traders, and argued the case for international trade on a basis of complete *laissez-faire*. Nowadays, this is no longer the position, and most capitalist economists accept the necessity of some degree of regulation. Some of them are protectionists, and favour regulation by tariff because this method leaves business men to adjust their transactions to the tariff without any further control over their operations. Some accept, usually with regret and with the hope that the need will disappear, quantitative forms of regulation by means of quotas, licences, or rationing of foreign exchange. Most recognise the need for the State, or for the Central Bank, to pay attention to the international balance of payments. Even, however, when such expedients are accepted as necessary, they are usually, among economists, still regarded as exceptional and as forced on a country only because the mechanism of free exchanges is not working properly. This does not apply to the out-and-out protectionists, who believe that a country can best increase the volume of employment by keeping out competitive foreign goods and thus enabling home manufacturers to charge higher prices. But this type of protectionism, though common among business men and politicians, does not find much favour with British economists, who have usually recognised that there can be no logical case for tariff protection that does not also extend to other forms of regulation of foreign trade and sometimes to a degree of economic planning which most of them are very unwilling to admit. Nevertheless, the decay of free trade doctrine and the growing endorsement of protectionism and of regulation of the balance of payments have carried many capitalist economists some distance towards the acceptance of the idea of planning in the field of international commerce.

Where foreign trade is planned between countries, each participating country agrees to take so much of certain kinds of each other's products and to pay for what it takes either with its own exports or with credits that can be used in buying from other sources. Such agreements are made for periods of time, which should be long enough to facilitate effective planning of production. They embody either fixed prices for standardised goods, or terms and conditions for settling the ratios of exchange between the goods affected. Usually, for standardised products, they involve arrangements for bulk sale and bulk purchase through state trading agencies, which can also build up in concert buffer stocks of primary products of which the annual supply fluctuates widely from natural causes. For less standardised goods and services, where these methods are inapplicable, countries can make trading bargains by agreeing to produce and supply defined goods or services which the other countries want, and the exchanges can be financed by mutual grants of credits expendable by each country in the country from which supplies are drawn or in other countries which belong with it to a common currency group.

It is not necessary to plan *all* international trade. Indeed, the right way of beginning is clearly to plan internationally the national shares in the production of such things as lend themselves most easily to such treatment, and therewith the quantities to be imported and exported as between the countries concerned—and thereafter, on a basis of experience, gradually to extend the method to more commodities and to additional countries.

The extent to which a country is prepared to rely on imports for things essential to the very life of its people is bound to depend on the degree of security it feels that supplies will not be cut off, either by war of from any other cause. Furthermore, no country can afford to import more than it is in a position to pay for, unless it receives the excess as a sheer gift. It can *temporarily* buy more, by running into debt ; but this will decrease its ability to import in the future, unless the loans can be used to bring about a more than equivalent increase in its own production. Therefore, apart from gifts and from loans used to good effect for productive purposes, a country needs to limit its imports to what it can pay for with its own exports of goods and services (or out of sums already owing to it from abroad). The Free Trade system offers no assurance either that imports will be limited to the required extent in the short run or that in the long run the society will be able to import even the things that are indispensable for the maintenance of its way of life. The orthodox Free Trader's answer to this latter problem is that, if a country cannot sell enough exports to buy the imports its population needs, that is a sign [1] that its population is too large, and that some of them ought to emigrate to more efficient countries in which there is an expanding demand for man-power. But (a) emigration is a highly selective progress, which removes mainly the more vigorous members of a society, leaving the old and the less productive behind, and (b) men are not commodities, to be bundled about the world in obedience to economic forces without regard for their feelings and love of home. A country which cannot pay with exports for all the goods it needs that can be produced more advantageously elsewhere in terms of cost and effort may need to produce some of these goods at home at higher cost. It should, however, seek to escape from such a situation by finding forms of production which will enable it to meet the cost of imports with less effort than is needed for producing substitutes for them at home.

In planned international specialisation and exchange there are real difficulties in the way of settling what are fair ratios for the exchange of products—e.g. foodstuffs or raw materials as against exports of manufactured goods. It is not really possible to measure the relative 'real costs' of producing these things in comparative terms. The measures used under capitalism begin by taking as a basis the money costs, including wages in the various countries; but such costs in fact result from, fully as much as they cause, the prices at which goods are valued. If the real wage in Malaya is low, this is a factor in making

---

[1] Except in the case of an overvalued currency, resulting in too high a price-level for exports, in which case a remedy may be found in devaluation.

rubber cheap; but the cheapness of rubber is also a factor in keeping wages, and therefore costs of production, low in Malaya. Hitherto, in general, peasant and native producers have been at a disadvantage in claiming higher incomes as against both capitalist employers and wage-workers in advanced countries; and peasant and plantation produce, except where the price of the latter has been artificially maintained by capitalist monopolies, have tended to be undervalued in comparison with industrial goods. The trend towards Socialism and against imperialist exploitation will help to correct this undervaluation and to enable the different types of producing countries to bargain on more equal terms. An advanced socialist country will be prepared to revise its valuation of peasant or native produce in terms of its own goods as part of an effort to raise standards of living throughout the world, even if this revaluation reacts to some extent to its own disadvantage; but no country will be prepared to do this to a greater extent than it thinks it can bear without national disaster. Accordingly we must expect the advance towards Socialism to be accompanied by uncertainties about the ratios of exchange between primary and manufactured products, the extent of the requisite revaluation depending on the speed at which productive efficiency develops in the more backward countries as a result of improved purchasing power and of technical help from the more advanced countries.

11. Socialist Economics, like the classical Economics of the capitalist epoch, rest on a world-wide pursuit of economic ends. But, whereas the older classical economists, in formulating their main doctrines, practically ignored national frontiers and thought in terms of transactions between individual business men and of free movements both of goods and money and of human beings across frontiers in search of economic opportunities, the

modern economist has to pay regard to national groups. This applies particularly to socialist economists for two main reasons—(a) because unified world-wide planning is for the present clearly impossible, and the only practicable form of socialist planning must rest upon national planning units and mutual arrangements between such units; and (b) because the Socialist is not prepared to accept a system which ignores men's attachment to their homeland and their demand to be given a living income and social security for working within it, unless they are prepared *voluntarily* to go elsewhere.

World-wide planning, by a unitary authority in control of the development of resources throughout the world, is conceivable only on a foundation of World Government. But World Government is too remote a prospect to be taken into account in considering the organisation of international economic relations. It is therefore necessary to assume a world divided politically into a number of national or regional units, and to base socialist economic policies on planning within and between these units. This does not, of course, exclude closer—even federal—relations between some of these units than overall; but it does involve thinking of world planning as a process of co-ordinating and reconciling national or regional plans, each concerned primarily with the well-being of the peoples immediately planned for, and only in the second place with that of other peoples. No doubt, ideally, we should all put the welfare of every person in the world on a par with that of ourselves and our fellow-citizens; but Socialists are no more likely than other moralists to be in a position to act politically in this ideally moral way. The most that can be hoped for, under present conditions, is that Socialists will be prepared to give greater weight than has been given in the past to the claims of international fellowship, and to devote more effort to making their plans fit in with the requirements of other countries and with the will to co-operate closely in efforts to improve standards of living throughout the world.

In practice, international planning for welfare and for the fruitful division of labour among the peoples can exist only on a basis of national planning. But national planning has its dangers wherever the will to adjust national plans to international requirements is weak or wanting. The Nazis were 'national planners', and high protectionism for national industries has been, to the world's loss, all too common a feature of such 'national planning' as has existed under capitalism. In socialist Economics the presumption is in favour of carrying planning by international agreement to the furthest point compatible with the full employment of home resources. The aim of socialist planners should be always to seek to transcend the limitations of purely national planning by the conclusion of agreements for the concerted planning not only of trade but also of productive investment and development policies on a supra-national basis.

This principle has special applications in the field of foreign investment. The economically backward countries can raise their standards of living in face of rapidly increasing populations only if they get external help in adding to their capital equipment. This applies not only or even mainly to manufacturing industries; it applies still more to agricultural equipment, to transport equipment, and to public utility development—e.g. irrigation and electric power. It is a principle of socialist Economics that the more advanced countries should help the less advanced with loans for the purchase of capital equipment, not on usurious terms or so as to exploit the cheap labour of the backward countries, but on generous conditions and in the hope of reaping the reward, not in high direct returns, but through the increased productivity and mutually advantageous international trade that will result from a rise in the efficiency of the less advanced peoples.

12. Finally, socialist Economics are essentially humanitarian. They are conceived from start to finish in terms of the promotion of human welfare. They are not a mere examination of the workings of an economic order regarded as existing independently of men's wills, but a purposive study designed to indicate the best means of shaping the factors that are not humanly controllable by the use of those that are. For this purpose it is necessary to study the facts objectively, and to observe what limitations on man's shaping power are implicit in the nature of the forces with which he has to deal. This study includes that of man himself, both in his behaviour as a productive agent and in his habits and reactions as a consumer. It also includes that of the social structure as a whole, in which the economic structure is inextricably embedded : the economic aspects can be fruitfully separated out for study only if it is continually kept in mind that such study involves an abstraction from the living unity of social life. These and other cognate studies of fact form an essential part of socialist Economics ; but they figure in it only as data of which account must be taken in the framing of practical policies for the furtherance of human welfare in its economic aspects.

Of course, some of these postulates would be accepted, wholly or in part, by many economists who are not Socialists but Keynesians or adherents of the Pigou school of ' Welfare Economics.' I said at the very beginning of this book that socialist Economics have much in common with non-socialist Economics, because they deal largely with the same problems; and obviously this applies most to those non-socialists who are concerned to find cures for the most evident defects of the economic system from the standpoints of high production and human welfare. I particularly wish non-socialist readers to ask themselves at this point how many, or how much, of my postulates they accept, and socialist readers to consider how much of them they could not accept unless they were Socialists.

I think most non-socialists will say they accept Postulate 1.[1] But do they? It involves rejecting the idea that an act of production is worth while if it means more disutility to the producers than satisfaction to the consumers of the particular thing produced. It therefore involves that much production is worth while only if the system of distribution is such as to maximise the satisfactions derived from it; for by the law of diminishing utility the more a consumer has of a thing the less satisfaction he derives from the average unit. Thus, when distribution is seriously unequal, the disutility of producing the later units may be greater than the utility realised in their consumption.

Again, some non-socialists will say they accept Postulate 2[2]; but do they really accept the basic assumption of equal economic *rights*?

Postulate 3[3] no doubt many non-socialists will accept, as far as words go. But will they act on it?

Postulate 4,[4] as far as it relates to industrial democracy, very few non-socialists and, alas! by no means all who call themselves Socialists will accept.

Postulate 5[5] is a matter rather of degree of acceptance than of absolute acceptance or rejection. Welfare economists who are not Socialists, such as Lord Beveridge, will accept much of it, but not, I think, the whole.

Postulate 6[6] will be broadly accepted by Keynesians and by most exponents of welfare economics. It is not in itself distinctively socialist, though acting fully on it is.

[1] See p 56. [2] See p. 57. [3] See p. 58. [4] See p. 59. [5] See p. 61. [6] See p. 62.

THE POSTULATES OF SOCIALIST ECONOMICS

Similarly, Postulate 7 [1] will be acceptable in the main to many non-socialist advocates of economic planning; but will they mean the same as I mean by " social and democratic ' determination of the volume of investment and consumption ?

In Postulate 8 [2] the main difference will turn upon two points—the definition of a ' minimum living income ' and the amount of inequality of income requisite to secure adequate incentives.

Postulate 9 [3] will, I think, be rejected by nearly all— perhaps by all—non-socialists.

Postulate [4] 10 will be accepted in some degree by non-socialist ' planners '; but few, if any, non-socialists will accept its full implications.

Postulate 11 [5] will be partly accepted by many non-socialists, but rather as an improvement and regrettable necessity than as a basic principle of human welfare.

Finally, Postulate 12 [6] will probably be widely endorsed, as far as the words go, but only Socialists will act on it. Moreover, many who cannot deny its truth will nevertheless dislike it, because it rejects the possibility of making Economics a science divorced from considerations of welfare in a wider sense than the purely ' economic welfare ' which most theoretical economists now admit into their calculations.

These paragraphs may appear to indicate a surprising amount of common ground between Socialists and ' non-socialist progressives.' But the proof of the pudding is in the eating. Socialists not merely accept these postulates: they also act on them—in the main.

[1] See p. 63. [2] See p. 65. [3] See p. 68. [4] See p. 69. [5] See p. 74. [6] See p. 77.

CHAPTER IV

PLANNING, EMPLOYMENT AND PRODUCTION

THE classical economists and their orthodox successors habitually treated the highest possible production as the unquestioned purpose of economic activity. Setting out from the conception of human wants which this activity was to satisfy within the limits of what could be produced, they asserted that system to be best that would issue in the highest possible total of goods and services. As goods and services of different sorts cannot be simply added together, some indirect way of measuring and comparing them had to be used, and this was found in the prices which they fetched in the market. This involved assuming that every offer of the same amount of money for any good or service represented an equal 'want,' so that the thing for which the amount was paid had a corresponding 'value.' The greater the sum of all the money prices paid for all the goods and services sold, the greater, on this showing, appeared to be the total 'value' created, and therefore the total production. But of course, the classical economists could not really mean this; for they were well aware that money prices are affected by the amount of purchasing power available, and did not suppose that, if prices rose without any change in the quantities of goods and services produced, there was any real increase in value or production. They had to invent a notion of 'real value,' as distinct from the expression of value in money terms, based on the amount of expected satisfaction represented by the purchaser's offer of a certain proportion of the available supply of purchasing power. Some later economists tried to get away from this notion of 'real value,' by insisting that they studied only market prices and did not attempt to go beyond them; but in practice these economists too had often to make use of a substitute for 'real value,' by valuing goods and services at the prices of a particular year, or other period—a device without which they were unable to arrive at any measurement of the production of one year as against another.

If the total supply of money available for buying things is taken as fixed, every price represents a proportion of this total, and it *can* be assumed that all prices express *relative* valuations of the goods and services for which they are paid—relative, that is, to the valuations of other things. This process of relative valuation is indeed the essential characteristic of the price system. Every purchaser must think what he buys worth to him at least what he pays for it in the light of the total sum he has to spend and of the prices asked for other things, or he would refrain from buying it. Doubtless, some purchasers buy things for a good deal less than they would be prepared to pay rather than go without; and some economists —notably Alfred Marshall—have made great play with the notion of a 'consumer's surplus' which accrues to those whom market conditions enable to buy things for less than they would have been ready to pay. The difficulty attending this notion is that people cannot in fact offer for everything they wish to buy more than their total incomes, so that what they are prepared to offer for one thing depends on what they have to offer for other things. The conception of consumer's surplus is indeed unhelpful and largely unreal [1]; and we can be content

[1] Consumer's surplus is often regarded as the difference between the price paid by the consumer for the final unit of a thing that he buys and the higher prices he would have been prepared to pay for the previous units. Thus, if I would buy 1 orange at 1s., 2 at 10d. each, 3 at 8d., 4 at 6d., 5 at 4d. and 6 at 2d., it is argued that I am really getting, when I buy 6 for 1s. the lot, a value equal to 2d.+4d.+6d.+8d.+10d.+1s.=3s. 6d. But this is nonsense. The first orange is worth 1s. to me only if I have not got the other five, and so on. The six cannot be worth to me much more than 1s., or I should buy more. Moreover, a great many purchases are not divisible into units in this simple way. If I buy only one of a thing, this

with the proposition that every purchase, unless it be made under compulsion, implies a personal valuation of the thing purchased as worth the sum paid for it. It is, however, quite illegitimate to extend this statement from the individual to the whole economy, on the assumption that every shilling paid for a thing represents the same amount of expected satisfaction. A shilling forms a much higher proportion of a poor man's than of a rich man's total income; and a rich man may be willing to pay a higher price for a thing than a poor man can afford, even if the rich man's expectation of satisfaction from getting it is much less than the poor man's.

The importance of this point for Economic Theory is obvious. If every shilling paid for a thing did represent an equal expectation of satisfaction—i.e. an equal want— it would be legitimate to conclude that selling everything to the highest bidders would ensure the largest total satisfaction of wants, and further that the bids of would-be consumers would influence the producers to supply the market with more-wanted as against less-wanted things, and so would tend to promote the highest possible production of wanted goods and services. Even so, there would be of course no assurance that production would be adapted to real needs, as distinct from undifferentiated wants; for consumers might prefer to spend their incomes foolishly. But there would at least be a strong presumption that people were getting what they thought they wanted most, rather than what they wanted less, or not at all.

In fact, however, the price system, under what are

---

kind of consumer's surplus cannot come in, though I may be paying for the one thing less than I should have been prepared to pay rather than go without it. The entire notion rests on a double mistake; for it is assumed (a) that *every* successive dose of a thing has a less value to the consumer than each preceding dose, which is not true until a reasonably satisfying quantity has been acquired, and (b) that each dose can be valued separately, unaffected by the possession or non-possession of the others. Attempts have been made recently to rehabilitate the notion of ' consumer's surplus ' in a new guise; but I think the criticism of it remains valid.

called 'free market conditions,' weights the scales all the time in favour of the possessors of large incomes, as against the relatively poor. It does not measure one man's wants against other men's wants on any basis that recognises the equality of the persons concerned. It serves as a means whereby the individual can make the best of his income within the structure of prices by distributing his purchases according to the relative urgency of his wants ; but it does not even begin to ensure that one man's greater want will be satisfied in preference to another man's lesser want. It gives the rich man a power to influence production that is denied to his poorer neighbours : it rests on the assumption that the proper claimants to satisfactions are shillings, and not men.

This might be regarded as right and proper if it could be taken for granted both that some men have superior claims to have their wants satisfied and also that the actual distribution of incomes coincides with the extent of these claims. At the period when Political Economy first became a subject of study the first of these two assumptions was regarded almost as a social axiom, not merely on grounds of superior service meriting a higher return, but also, as we saw, of a prescriptive right of the members of certain privileged classes. The economists did not positively defend the claims of the privileged, though they went out of their way to attack them only in special cases : they did, however, most energetically defend the claims based on superiority of service, and included with these the claim to a return on capital, identifying the capital with the capitalist and endorsing the capitalist's claim to treat the services of 'his' capital as his own. They sought, moreover, to demonstrate that in a 'free market economy' each 'factor of production' —land, labour, capital and enterprise—would tend to receive a reward corresponding to its 'productivity'; a reward which would accrue to its owner. Thus, the superior purchasing power of some men over others would correspond to superior service, and would represent the claim of the superiors to have more of their wants satisfied than other men.

This claim, when stripped of its false identification of the 'service' of land or capital with the 'service' of the person who owns it, may be valid, as applicable to differences of earned income, as far as such differences do correspond to amounts of service rendered. This makes nonsense, however, of the contention that the 'free market economy' ensures the prior satisfaction of the more urgent wants, and thus tends to maximise total satisfaction. For, even if it is proper to pay a man more for better service, the effect of doing so is to give him a claim to have some of his less urgent wants satisfied in preference to some of the more urgent wants of poorer persons : so that the whole idea of maximising total satisfactions goes by the board. There is no possibility of arguing that the urgency or intensity of men's wants corresponds either to the amount or quantity of their service or to the size of their incomes. It is simply not the nature of the 'free market economy' to ensure maximum production in any intelligible sense of the term ; for as soon as we cease to assume that products of different sorts can be fairly measured one against another by their relative prices, the entire basis for measuring total production is knocked away.

It remains, no doubt, possible, very approximately and over fairly short periods, to measure broad *changes* in total production from time to time, provided that the limitations of such index number methods are fully allowed for. It also remains possible, of course, to measure the output of particular things which are capable of bulk measurement ; but even in such cases very misleading conclusions may be reached by ignoring differences of quality, and there is no really valid means of reducing qualitative to quantitative differences. Less standardised products can be aggregated only by using the delusive measure of price, or sometimes the hardly less delusive measure of man-power (or man-power and material) used in producing them. It is not really possible to make estimates of total production except by adding up the prices of all the products and then, when comparisons are to be made over time, adjusting the total by dividing by some factor representing that elusive conception—the 'general level of prices.' Such estimates have their uses; but it is entirely illegitimate to regard them as estimates of total satisfaction afforded, or to say that whatever aggregate of diverse products can be sold for the highest total price must be the aggregate yielding the highest total satisfaction of wants. If purchasing power had been differently distributed among the people, the relative money demand for different things would have altered, and a different aggregate of goods and services would have commanded the highest total price; but there is no evidence, derivable from the price-system, to show which of these aggregates would have yielded the larger total of satisfactions. Yet, unless satisfactions can be measured and equated with 'demands,' on what ground can the highest possible production be taken as the end of economic action and, indeed, what real meaning can the words be supposed to possess?

Of course, I am not suggesting that we cannot in practice tell when a society is increasing its aggregate production, and even roughly at what rate. What I am saying is that such measurements as we can use for this purpose are never absolute, but always relative to a particular social-economic structure. They reflect and are conditioned by the scales of value recognised in each particular society. They are derived from the distribution of incomes prevailing in it, and thus depend on the maintenance substantially unaltered of the weightings which the system in fact gives to different persons' wants. Now, a society moving towards Socialism, with its preference for as near an approach to equality as seems practicable under the existing conditions, will obviously weight different men's wants in a different scale from that appropriate to a capitalistic society, and will be continually re-making its scale as it gets nearer to a fully socialist system.

The old Economics took wants into account only when they appeared in the market reinforced by purchasing power. What counted was the willingness of buyers to spend money on things—and their having it to spend: nothing else. Of course, individuals were not the only spenders: there were also firms and corporations, spending collectively both on capital goods and materials and intermediate products and on labour; and there were the State and local public bodies, spending on the public services—armaments and forces pay, schools and teachers' salaries, health services, and so on. Public and private spending counted alike, according to their money amount, in making up the total of demand, which included demands for capital goods as well as for consumers' goods and services, and demands for labour in all its forms as well as demands for materials, fuel, and goods at various intermediate stages of manufacture. All these demands came together, and were in some degree competitors in the market, which was really a series of interrelated markets for different kinds of things. No want counted at all for the economist unless it was backed by an offer of purchasing power. No doubt, the public authorities, to the extent to which they maintained services which used up scarce resources, were partly actuated by a sense of people's *needs*, and set out to satisfy some *wants* which would otherwise have failed to be translated into market demand because of the poverty of those who felt them or because they seemed to some people less compelling than other wants which used up all their purchasing power.

The public authorities might even decide to satisfy certain *needs* which most of its individual citizens did not recognise as *wants* of their own—e.g. in the fields of higher education or preventive medicine ; and where this was done, these *needs*, being backed by public purchasing power, would rank equally in the market with any other form of 'effective demand.' The greater part of the total spending, however, on all kinds of purchases has been done in capitalist societies by private persons or business firms ; and, if we set aside for the moment purchases of capital goods, intermediate goods, and such services as transport for business purposes, and also set aside the quite special case of purchases of productive labour in all its forms, we can say that the bulk of what is left—i.e. spending on finished consumers' goods and on consumers' services—is likely to continue to be effected in the same way in a socialist society. Some goods and services the public authorities will no doubt supply ' free of charge '—that is, by paying for them out of public revenue rather than charging the individual recipients for them ; and the total range of such ' free ' services may become wider as society advances towards Socialism. But it will be agreed that in a socialist society the individual consumer ought to be given a wide range of choice in spending the bulk of the income society can afford to allow him, and that in some respects a nearer approach to economic equality may make it less necessary to supply things ' free ' in order to ensure that no one goes without them for reasons of poverty or ignorance of their virtues. Given a good basic minimum income for all, the question whether a service can best be rendered ' free ' or charged for to the individual recipient will come to be one rather of social convenience than of redressing inequalities in ability to pay. Indeed, the more recent extensions of the social services—insurance and assistance benefits, children's allowances, and so on—have taken largely the form of cash payments which the recipient is free to spend as he pleases. This involves a recognition of the high value of 'consumer's choice,' and of the fact that most poor people can be trusted, in such a society as ours, to put the freedom of choice to good use in accordance with the purposes for which the allowances are made.

Cash allowances reinforce the purchasing power of poor people in accordance with the conception of need, while allowing the recipients freedom in spending the money. Thus, they reinforce the free consumers' market. whereas allowances in kind, though they equally take goods off the market and involve expenditure of purchasing power, restrict freedom of choice. A socialist, or a socialistic, society will have continually to consider where to draw the line between supplying things 'free'—which means paying for them out of taxes or compulsory contributions—and adjusting incomes so as to allow the main body of consumers to make their own choices over a wider range. In general, it seems likely that the method of 'free' supply will be carried further and further in the fields of education, health, and various kinds of public amenity, and also in such special cases as the provision of school meals and milk, which are closely related to both education and health, but that in most other fields the maintenance and effective widening of individual choice will be deemed preferable to any sort of compulsion to consume one thing rather than another.

This means that, in planning the national production and the investment which governs its future development, the responsible planners of a socialist society will be in the main, not deciding what people ought to want, but responding to popular demand. The demand for consumers' goods and services will reflect the changed distribution of incomes resulting from the adoption of a national minimum policy and from other social service developments ; and the planners' task in relation to production will be to ensure that, as far as possible, the pattern of supply corresponds to the consumers' willingness to pay. If demand for some things looks like expanding, and demand for other things looks like falling off, it will be for the planners to devise means of increasing supply through investment and attraction and training of workers in the former fields, and to decrease investment and check labour recruitment in the latter. This means, of course, that the planners will be seeking, just as business men do under capitalism, to anticipate the course of demand for some time ahead—for how long must depend on the time needed for the necessary adaptations of the economic structure.

Thus the 'price system' will continue to exist under Socialism, and will serve the important function of enabling the consumers to exercise free choice in the allocation of their limited total incomes among alternative uses. There is nothing wrong with the price system as such: what is wrong with its working under capitalism is that, with incomes badly distributed, it distorts instead of reflecting the needs and wants of the people. Given a reasonably satisfactory distribution of incomes, the price system is obviously the most sensible instrument for ensuring that each individual shall get what he wants, subject only to the insistence of the State that he shall have some things (such as education) whether he wants them or not, and shall have certain other things (such as dangerous drugs) either not at all or only at a deterrent price. The reason why the prices offered for goods fail to reflect the satisfactions expected from possessing them is that men's incomes in no way correspond to their appetites. Put right the weighting of demand by improving the distribution of incomes, and much that economists have written falsely about the working of the price system under capitalism will at last come true.

Of course, this implies that, in the absence of special

reasons for making particular products artificially cheap or dear—by subsidies or by indirect taxation—the prices of goods and services under Socialism will be based on costs. If prices were fixed arbitrarily, without any relation to costs, there would be no assurance of fair dealing in the matter of consumers' choice. What the consumer has a right to require is that, broadly speaking, every shilling he spends shall represent a call on a shillingsworth of real factor cost—that is, the using up of a shillingsworth of productive power. But this can be the case only if prices bear a clear relation to costs of production.

'But how', ask a number of economists hostile to Socialism, ' how will it be possible for a socialist economy correctly to interpret the consumers' wishes? Consumers' demand is not something absolute; it depends on prices as well as on incomes—on the relative prices asked for different things as well as on the absolute prices. Will not the socialist planners, if they fix or influence the prices charged for the various goods and services, be therewith influencing the structure of consumers' demands?' Of course they will: every price has a demand level corresponding to it at any particular time: there is no such thing as demand—though there are want and need—irrespective of price. Accordingly, fixing prices *is* fixing demand, at any given level and distribution of incomes and in any given condition of consumers' tastes and preferences.

But on what principles will the socialist planners fix prices, or influence their levels, if they mean in the main to follow, rather than to form, consumers' demands? Certainly they will not wish to do this arbitrarily: they will be attempting, as we have seen, to secure that prices shall conform to costs of production, which will of course vary according to the scale of output and to the varying effects of higher and lower output on the unit costs of producing different things. For most manufactured goods, given time to instal the requisite equipment, unit costs tend to fall rapidly with increasing output ; whereas no such generalisation holds good in the case of primary products, except with important qualifications. The more consumers' wants can be met by larger supplies of things that can be produced at decreasing cost, the more satisfactions are likely to accrue ; but this does not mean that consumers ought to be put off with enlarged supplies of cheaper goods which, after taking account of the price, they want less than more expensive goods. The planners can legitimately try to stimulate demand for what can be produced most easily in greater quantity at lower cost ; but they must stop short of forcing such goods on a reluctant public that would sooner buy something else if it were available.

Let us try to see as clearly as we can what this social planning of production in relation to consumers' needs involves. There exists at any time an actual structure of prices, to which consumers accommodate their purchases. This structure is not fixed : some parts of it change frequently, others much more slowly ; and the consumers are continually adapting their purchases to these changes, as well as to changes in their own incomes and scales of preference. Their wants, as well as their means of satisfying them, alter, and are influenced by fashion, advertisement, and many other factors besides changing prices. The socialist planners of production will thus find themselves confronted with an actual state of demand for the various kinds of goods and services, corresponding to an actual structure of incomes and prices ; and they can to some extent estimate the probable effects of changes in both prices and the level and distribution of consumers' incomes on the demand for different things. Of course they cannot do this exactly ; and their ability to do it varies greatly from one thing to thing. But they can do it at least as well as an association of capitalist firms and a great deal better than most individual firms; and in particular they have two advantages which the individual firm usually lacks. In the first place, their calculations cannot be upset by the action of other producers of whose output plans they are ignorant,[1] this being an advantage which is also at the disposal of the complete monopolist under capitalism. Secondly, they will know about any planned changes in the output of substitutes or in the distribution of spendable incomes. With these advantages they will be better placed than any capitalist producer for anticipating the effects on demand of changing the prices charged for goods and services as well as the probable future demand at the existing prices.

A highly elastic demand for a thing, given a suitable distribution of incomes and a lack of noxiousness in the thing itself, is a valid reason for increasing the supply whenever this can be done at decreasing unit cost. The planners, just as they will be faced with an existing structure of prices, will be faced with a parallel structure of costs, dependent on the payments made for the use of the 'factors of production' employed in providing the existing supply and on the efficiency with which these factors are employed. Changes in the payments made for the use of the factors will affect these costs; and so will changes in the efficiency of their use. But the cost of each unit will be affected by the scale of output in varying ways for different products and over short and long periods. The aim of the planners will be to respond to the consumers' demands by taking every opportunity to increase the efficiency and thus lower the unit costs of production; but they will be right in endeavouring to stimulate consumers' latent demand for products which

[1] Even if there is a 'private sector' in competition with public enterprise, the planners will know about its productive capacity and about what it is intending to produce. I am by no means assuming that under Socialism *all* production will be planned by a central authority—only that the central authority will have knowledge of other people's plans in making its own.

PLANNING, EMPLOYMENT AND PRODUCTION 93

can be produced at lower unit cost[1] as total output is increased. Neither under Capitalism nor under Socialism can output be merely a response to an existing structure of demand. There is always a necessary element of fostering potential demand by the offer of new kinds of goods and services or of existing kinds at lower prices; and it is important that this process shall be directed to eliciting the latent demands that can be most easily supplied. This does not mean that socialist planners should thrust on the public commodities which the public does not want; but it does mean that the public cannot fully know what it does want until things are actually offered for sale. If the planners mistakenly expect an expanding demand which does not accrue even at a reduced price, that is just too bad; but the same kind of mistake occurs under Capitalism, and socialist planners, with fuller knowledge, are both less likely to make it and in a better position to correct it than the capitalist producer can usually be.

It may be objected that this is not so because the planners, when they do make mistakes, will usually do so on a bigger scale than capitalist producers. But why should this be so? Under Capitalism, except where full monopoly exists, errors of judgment are commonly multiplied because competing producers are ignorant of one another's production plans. Socialist planners will be able to experiment with fuller knowledge, and to try

[1] I am well aware that some economists consider that the governing factor in deciding how much of each commodity to produce should be *marginal* and not *average* unit cost. This would mean that industries producing under conditions of increasing marginal cost would make profits and industries producing under conditions of decreasing marginal costs would make losses. (Marginal cost of course means the additional cost involved in making a small additional quantity.) This view is upheld by asserting that as long as the value, measured by sale price, of the additional output exceeds the additional cost of making it, there must be a net gain in utility. But this need not be so if the acquisition of the additional output lessens the unit utility of what was previously produced, as it may well do. For the reason for this, see the footnote on 'consumer's surplus' on page 81.

out the effects of a moderate expansion of supply before embarking on larger ventures. Capitalist monopolists make fewer mistakes of this sort than are made under competitive conditions: they are indeed more prone to under-estimate than to over-estimate the expansibility of demand. Why should it be supposed that socialist planners will tend to rush to the opposite extreme? Too much caution, rather than undue venturesomeness, is much more likely to be their besetting sin.

In general, then, the planners will be arranging for production on the understanding that the products will be priced according to the unit costs of producing the quantities that are to be made, and will be trying to get produced the quantities which consumers will be ready to buy at such prices. But at this point a further objection is raised. How, under a socialist system, will the costs of production themselves be determined? Under capitalist conditions, costs depend partly on the prices paid for the ' factors of production '—land, capital, labour and enterprise (or management); and the owners of these factors compete in the market for what they can get in return for their services: so that, for the business firm, costs have an *objective* aspect, though they are of course also affected by the efficiency with which the factors are utilised after they have been bought or hired. Under Socialism, however, the prices to be paid for the use of the ' factors of production ' will no longer be determined by this market competition, but will be at any rate largely settled by the planning authority as a matter of public policy. Wages, for example, whatever the precise methods of determining them—to which we shall come later—will clearly not be left entirely to the higgling of the market, either individually, or by trial of strength between powerful Trade Unions and the employers—public or private—in charge of the conduct of the various industries and services. Even apart from the general application of a minimum standard, which will affect the entire wage structure, there will have to be means of relating the remuneration of particular groups to the total sum available for payment as wages and salaries to all the producers; and this will involve some say of the public authorities in the distribution of this total among rival claimants.

It must, I think, be admitted that, if the competition of the market for labour is rejected as a means of assessing claims to wages, on the ground that if neither furnishes a true measure of services rendered nor produces effects in conformity with social needs, there is only one theoretical alternative way in which services could be weighed objectively one against another, so as to determine the appropriate *relative* payments for different types of work. This would be some form of the so-called 'points system' advocated by some consulting engineers, who have proposed that the skill and effort involved in each type of work should be scientifically assessed by experts. So many 'points' would then be assigned to each job, and relative wages would be fixed on this basis without any need for collective bargaining or any appeal from the expert's judgment. I regard this proposal with the utmost suspicion. I know of no scientific basis on which any such assessment could be made, even between closely related jobs; and to propose it as a means of valuing every kind of work—or even of wage-labour—in relation to every other seems to me fantastically absurd. It is the old fallacy of Taylorism, in its most extreme form, dressed up afresh in the garments of pseudo-science.

If this alternative is rejected, as I am sure it must be, we are thrown back on common sense—and there are many worse things to come to rest on. I do not believe that there is any way—either market competition or any other—of fixing relative wages so as to make them correspond exactly to the amount of service rendered. I do not accept—and no Socialist can accept—the view of the older economists that this result is sufficiently secured by market competition for labour, with or without Trade Unions, or that the relative wages arrived at by this method are worthy of any respect as furnishing a rational basis for the reckoning of real costs. I believe sheer common sense, applied by arbitrators who have listened to the arguments put forward by the parties concerned, will yield as good a basis for the fixing of wage-rates as it is possible to secure, provided only that three conditions are satisfied :—

(*a*) that the arbitrators shall be not ' efficiency experts ' but persons chosen for common sense ;

(*b*) that they shall work not in isolation, dealing quite separately with each case as it comes up, but in concert, so as to be able to compare the claims put forward in different occupations ; and

(*c*) that they shall pay some regard to the wage-differentials needed to secure the right supplies of labour for the various occupations, but shall also aim at reducing the need for such differentials by the use of alternative methods (e.g. training the right numbers for different jobs), and non-wage differentials, such as longer holidays, for adjusting the supply of each kind of labour to the demand.

(*d*) that they shall act within the framework of a general wage-policy based on the conception of a national minimum standard for all, and of a desire to keep inequalities within the limits set by the need to provide sufficient incentives to high output and by the sense of justice prevalent in the society at the time.[1]

See pp. 57 f. for the full statement of these principles.

This involves that, in a socialist society, wages, including both the national minimum standard and the rates applicable to particular occupations, will have to be settled by some central authority which has in view both the total amount available for distribution as wages and the broad principles on what occupational wage-differences are to be based.[1] With wages settled and adjusted in this way, I entirely deny that a socialist society would lack a 'rational' foundation for the estimating of factor-cost in respect of wages. On the contrary, it would have a much more rational foundation than has ever existed in capitalist society.

The principle here laid down in respect of wages and other earned incomes is no less applicable to the other factors of production. In capitalist societies, rates of interest have been for the most part in theory uncontrolled up to very recent times, and have been supposed by most economists to depend essentially on the same balance of supply and demand as other factor payments. It has, however, been necessary for even the strongest exponents of this view to recognise that at any rate one of the interacting forces—supply—has been much affected by monetary policy, which has been subject in varying degrees to public influence, through Treasuries if not through publicly controlled Central Banks. The simple view that the 'rate of interest' is determined by the willingness to save on the one hand and the willingness to borrow on the other is quite untenable, not only because, as Keynes first clearly showed, there is no necessary identity between what people are prepared to save and what *entrepreneurs* are prepared to borrow for investment, but

[1] Please note that I am speaking of a socialist society, or at least of a society largely advanced towards Socialism. It is not to be taken that I regard this method of wage-settlement as appropriate to the circumstances of Great Britain in 1950. Wage-regulation would need to be developed gradually, *pari passu* with the advance of socialisation and with the extension of control over other forms of income through taxation and other forms of economic regulation by the State.

also because the supply of capital available for borrowing depends on credit policy[1] as well as on saving, and because the readiness with which banks are prepared to advance money, as well as the interest rate they charge for it, affects investment.

It remains none the less true that, subject to certain conditions, the real investment a society can effect depends on the proportion of its productive capacity it is prepared to devote to this purpose as against spending on immediate consumption; but the assumed mutual exclusiveness of investment and consumption—the notion that so much more of the one means so much less of the other—holds good only on the assumption that *all* the available resources of production will be actually employed in one or other of the two alternative uses. If there are unemployed resources, it is possible to have more investment without reducing consumption, or *vice versa*, though in practice there may be obstacles because of the difficulty of transferring productive capacity from the one field to the other. If it could be simply a matter of deciding between alternative uses of a certain amount of productive capacity, by allowing the amount of new investment to be fixed by the effectiveness of offers of interest in inducing the possessors of incomes to save, there would be some sense in talking, as many economists have done, of a ' natural ' rate of interest, which would attract just the amount of capital wanted by borrowers at that rate. But such a situation bears hardly any resemblance to what has actually happened in any capitalist society. Actual rates of interest have, at any rate in the more advanced societies, been immensely affected both by government borrowing and government creation of means of payment and by the lending policy of both central and commercial banks. Rates of interest

---

[1] And on what Keynes called 'liquidity preference'—that is, a desire to hold 'cash' instead of buying things or shares with it, or locking it up over a long period.

PLANNING, EMPLOYMENT AND PRODUCTION

have always been largely arbitrary, in the sense of being settled by policy rather than by any self-acting economic law. Accordingly, the contention that public planning of production must be without any guidance as to the real cost of the capital which it directs to this or that particular use has no point ; for it applies fully as much to unplanned capitalist investment as to planned socialist investment.

No doubt, the readiness of individuals to save different amounts out of their incomes according as they can get higher or lower returns on their savings is one thing to be taken account of in fixing interest rates, as long as private savings are relied on for the provision of some of the capital that is deemed to be needed. Moreover, as long as investment (as distinct from saving) is left partly to the discretion of private persons who set out to borrow sums for capital development, the rate of interest such persons are called upon to pay is an influence affecting their willingness to borrow more or less. But these influences act in conjunction with many others ; and they cannot be treated as the two essential determinants of interest rates. Furthermore, to the extent to which the decision as to the amount of capital to be made available for investment is taken out of the hands of private persons, by the State itself assuming this deciding function, the amount saved by individuals becomes entirely irrelevant from the standpoint of settling investment policy. There may be nothing to prevent individuals, under such conditions, from saving out of their incomes as much or as little as they please : their saving less or more will affect, not the total sum available for investment, but only the proportion of that sum which has to be raised by taxation, or by some means other than saving out of personal incomes. Again, to the extent to which the State, as owner and administrator of industries, takes over the functions of the private business man or company, the willingness of such men or companies to borrow capital becomes irrelevant. Even in a 'mixed' economy, in which public and private sectors of industry exist side by side, but there is a general framework of overall planning for 'full employment,' the State, through its appropriate agencies, cannot escape the need to regulate interest rates in such a way that private borrowing takes up the amounts of new capital needed to enable the private sector to fulfil its part of the general economic plan. But for ensuring this the permitted margins of profit allowed by taxation policy and price-regulation are likely to be much more powerful instruments than the raising or lowering of interest rates.

This does not mean that interest will cease to exist or to be of importance in a socialist system. If two projects involve the same expenditures on labour and materials, but one will lock up capital in larger amount or for a longer period than the other, the project of which this is true will have a greater real cost, because it will divert more capital from alternative uses, or—which is the same thing—the same amount of capital for a longer time. The lock-up of real capital is a real cost, and needs to be represented in estimated costs in comparing the relative desirability of alternative projects. Thus, socialised enterprises can rightly be debited with an interest charge on the capital locked up in them, even where this capital is publicly owned and not borrowed from private persons. The rates of interest at which such accounting charges are made will need to be publicly determined, in relation to a 'general rate of interest' fixed by the public financial authorities (in effect the Central Bank acting in consultation with the Treasury).

Thus, in an economy broadly socialist, or at any rate dominated by some form of overall planning designed to promote full employment and social welfare, changes in interest rates are likely to be a matter of social expediency. Up to a point, the rates of interest fixed in such a society will be arbitrary—though hardly more so than such rates are under Capitalism, for they will be arbitrary only in the sense of being socially determined. They will be based not on the strange mixture of public and private influences which settles their level under capitalist conditions, but, broadly speaking, on a social judgment of what is desirable for the encouragement of private saving—if it is still to be encouraged when it has ceased to bear any relation to the quantity of investment—and on the degree of stimulus to, or deterrence from, large demands for capital which it is thought wise to apply to industrial and other borrowers public and private, in order to keep total investment at the planned level. It is to be presumed that publicly administered industries, whether they have to *pay* interest on capital invested in them or not, will be required to include in their estimated costs a charge for the use of the capital which they employ and thus take away from other possible uses; but the *rate* at which this charge is set down in their accounts will be fixed by the public authority, in the light of what is needed to maintain 'full employment,' and not of what will bring the willingness to save into balance with the willingness to invest. Moreover, in practice the scaling-up or scaling-down of demands for new capital in the main branches of production will be done directly, by the assignment of sums for capital investment to the various types of enterprise in accordance with the ability of the industries producing capital goods to deliver what is needed, as well as of the anticipated changes in consumers' demands for the various types of product, rather than by the clumsy instrument of varying interest rates on long-term capital.

Profit, in a largely socialised economy, will have two aspects—the actual profits realised in the industries and services still conducted as private enterprises, and the accounting surpluses over costs, including interest costs on capital, recorded by socialised industries and services—

or, of course, the corresponding losses or deficits. It can be assumed that socialised enterprises will be conducted, as far as possible, and subject to certain exceptions, on the assumption that their takings ought to cover their actual factor costs, and that where this rule is departed from for reasons of public policy any intentional deficits will be openly shown in the estimates as subsidies. Correspondingly, where for reasons of public policy products are sold well above cost (e.g. drink and tobacco) the excess due to this will continue to be skimmed off by taxation. I think it can be further assumed that in general permitted prices will be set at levels which will allow some surplus over current costs to be realised where socialised services are efficiently conducted, in order to enable such industries to have at their disposal some reserves for experiment, research and development work and some power to make minor investments of new capital without incurring additional interest charges on loans or advances from the State, or whatever may be the main source of new investment—e.g. a public Investment Board or Bank. If the State decides, as has been suggested earlier, to raise revenue for new investment mainly or largely by withdrawing purchasing power before it is distributed to consumers as income, prices will have to be set at a level high enough to cover this charge, which will be equivalent to some sort of general turnover tax.

The other kind of profit—that which will continue to accrue to the owners of businesses still in private hands—will obviously be related to the current rate of interest for long-term capital, but will include also a risk-element and an incentive-element designed to attract such investment as is desired by the planning authorities and to reward efficiency and penalise inefficiency. In the case of small owner-managed businesses it will also need to include a payment for management, involving a similar incentive-element. The incentive aspects of such payments will hardly differ in principle from the incentive-elements in wages and salaries, and will be similarly controlled, by price and tax policies, as part of the process of allocating incomes among the various classes of claimants. Thus, the profit-factor will become a controlled factor, and the need to offer high profit inducements will be lessened because there will no longer be any need to allow large profits to be made for the purpose of providing capital for business expansion. If a private business seeks to expand, except at a modest rate, it will have to secure the approval of the planning authorities for its investment projects and to secure the capital by borrowing either from the National Investment Board or from some other agency set up by the Government for the purpose, or from the public with the authority of the Board. This does not preclude allowing an efficient business to plough back part of the profit it makes into its own development; but it does mean that prices need not be allowed to be so high as they would have to be if reserved profits were to be regarded as the main source of expansion. The instruments for controlling profits in the private sector of the economy will be price-regulation and taxation; and of course, if taxes are imposed on industry generally for the financing of new capital development, the privately owned sector will be called upon to bear its share.

Rent of land raises a special problem. I assume that, at a fairly early stage of the advance towards Socialism, all land will be made public property, so that rents will be payable to the State—or possibly to regional authorities. How, then, will rents be fixed, when there is no longer more than a single supplier? The answer is again, as it was in the case of wages, by the exercise of common sense, with the difference that in the case of land there is no need for a 'national minimum.' Faced with many claimants for land, from farmers to industries, and from holiday camp agencies to housing authorities, a Land Board, or regional Land Boards, will be in a position to estimate the relative values of different patches of land and to assess reasonable rent charges. They will, however, hardly be guided exclusively by the same economic considerations as determine rents where land is in unrestricted private ownership. They will, for example, not rent good agricultural land for building development merely because a housing authority or an industrialist is prepared to offer a high price for its use, if there are alternative sites of lower agricultural value that can be adapted for the purposes of the proposed development. They will recognise that good agricultural land has a long-term value to society that is not measured by its economic rent. This principle is already recognised in town and country planning legislation ; and rent-fixing and land allocation in a socialist society will simply carry further the principles already established, though still very imperfectly applied. There will continue to be many bidders for the use of land, including public as well as private bidders, and the Land Board or Boards will respond to these bids in such a way as to take the wider aspects of public policy into account.

Thus, in a socialist economy, the sums paid for the use of the various factors of production, from labour to land, will be all controlled payments, related to a general plan designed both to achieve an *optimum* distribution of incomes from the standpoint of social welfare, subject to the state of popular opinion about the degree of inequality consistent with social justice, and also to provide sufficient incentives to efficiency and effort. These payments will be in a sense arbitrary, in that the planning authorities will be regulating them in order to promote ends which are regarded as socially desirable, and will not be merely following in a neutral spirit the dictates of any set of supposed economic laws. They will not be trying to behave ' as if '

Capitalism, and the 'free market' beloved of capitalist economists, were still in existence, but will be asking themselves, wherever the need for judgment arises, what the consequences of acting in this or that way are likely to be, and adopting the solution which, in all the circumstances, seems best calculated to promote the general welfare. This does not mean that they will be in a position to flout 'economic laws' at will : on the contrary, they will be responding to as well as moulding a structure of actual and prospective consumers' demand which it will be their principal function to satisfy as fully as the available resources allow. But they will have to do their own weighing of claim against claim, and of future needs against present demands. They will not be in a position to disregard the need for incentives in order to press the claims of equality to the limit, or to ignore the state of opinion about the standards of income appropriate to different callings ; but it will be their function, in the light of common sense and democratic intention, to weigh these considerations in the balance and to propose accommodations between conflicting objectives and attitudes.

In all the foregoing, wherever I have spoken of 'planning authorities,' I have of course had in mind not some board of supermen entitled to impose their judgment on society, but skilled and responsible agents, under the necessity of securing assent for their plans from Parliament and, finally, at the bar of public opinion. The expert planners will only propose: the representatives of the people must dispose, by accepting, modifying, or rejecting their proposals. I am not here discussing what should be the precise machinery for ensuring this responsibility ; for that question belongs to the realm of socialist Politics, rather than of socialist Economics.[1] That there should be democratic control over planning, in some effective form, is, however, an underlying assumption of all that I have written.

[1] On this question, see my small book, *The Machinery of Socialist Planning*.

CHAPTER V

ECONOMIC DEMOCRACY

Economic democracy has two aspects. In one aspect it is concerned with securing a high level of output and a distribution of goods and services approaching equality as nearly as can be made consistent with the need for incentives and with prevalent conceptions of social justice. In the other aspect it is concerned with the conditions under which production is done, and with the securing of as near an approach to equality among the producers as can be made consistent with the requirements of reasonably efficient industrial organisation. The demand for leisure cuts across this twofold division ; for leisure is wanted both as a release from labour and as an opportunity for enjoyment. It is both an abstinence from further economic effort and itself a form of consumption. Moreover, these two aspects of leisure are closely connected because the enjoyment of it, in many of its forms, involves the consumption of other things besides time—of house-room and furniture, of tennis racquets and golf clubs, balls, courts or courses, films and cinemas, books and papers, and a host of things besides. A man needs more goods and services when he has more leisure to enjoy them in ; and accordingly the balancing of the conflicting claims of higher production and greater leisure always raises difficult problems, even for a democracy which is seeking to diffuse both wealth and leisure as widely as possible, instead of granting the enjoyment of both to the few at the expense of overwork and poverty for the many.

Both the drive for profit through the production of more goods under conditions of decreasing cost and the manifest needs of the many poor for more consumers' goods and services have contributed to the tendency in Economics to put the emphasis on high output and almost to ignore the position of the producer except as a claimant to income. Not only the apologists of Capitalism but also many socialistic economists have written nearly as if they need, as economists, take no account of the conditions of production, except inasfar as they affect the output of goods and services. It is no doubt a part of the case for improving factory conditions and developing welfare and 'joint consultation' services that higher output often results from such measures, either directly or through the diminution of strikes and the prolongation of the period of working efficiency. But this is not the whole case ; and it may be desirable to improve the conditions of employment even where the effect will be to reduce production. This is now recognised, after long struggles, not only in the provisions of the Factory Acts and of other industrial laws laying down minimum requirements of factory hygiene and accident-prevention, but also in the statutory regulation of the length of the working day and week and in the recognition of Trade Union rights of collective bargaining as applied to the conditions of work. Hardly the less, economists tend to leave it out, except when they are considering its reactions upon costs, mainly because welfare condiderations are not measurable, as goods and services and personal incomes are, in terms of money prices. It is seldom possible to say by how much per cent a change in working conditions has decreased or increased the irksomeness of labour ; nor can falling or rising accident or sickness rates be measured against output on any common scale. It is possible to measure, at any rate in an approximate way, changes in the quantities of goods and services consumed, by using the none too accurate instrument of general index numbers for earnings and for living costs ; but there is no way of telling *how much* happier, or less happy, workers have been made either by changes in hours of work or conditions of working, or by being given, or refused, a share in determining such matters, or being more or less subject to tyranny or arbitrariness during their periods of employment.

That which cannot be weighed against other things in a common price scale, many economists have argued, can have no place in Economics, because Economics is essentially a measuring science with price as its standard of measurement. No Socialist can properly accept this view. It may be quite impossible to prove by any quantitative assessment that, say, a decrease in working hours that has been accompanied by a fall in total output has been worth while because the human satisfactions of greater leisure outweigh the loss of goods; but the lack of a comparative measuring-rod does not mean that it is possible to avoid weighing such things against each other, or that the one is a matter in which the economist should interest himself to the exclusion of the other. It would doubtless be much simpler if we could put everything to the test by means of a single kind of measurement, so as to be in a position to tell with certainty how to achieve the *optimum* total result. In the absence of such a standard we are not justified in dismissing from Economics everything that cannot be measured in terms of money payments. It is desirable and convenient to apply some method of measuring things whenever this can legitimately be done; and it is very convenient to be in a position to compare one thing with another by using a common measuring-rod. But there are dangers that, in pursuit of these conveniences, we may attempt to measure what cannot really be measured at all, or apply inappropriate methods of measurement in order to bring disparate things to a common account.

Worthwhileness is a matter of comparing the usefulness of results with the efforts and sacrifices involved in getting them, and also of comparing the usefulness of alternative results which make competing calls on the limited resources available for achieving them. In many instances, we know the cost of doing a thing—both the money cost and the real cost in materials and expenditure of man-power—but have no means of assessing quantitatively the usefulness of the result. This applies, for example, to most things that are publicly provided for collective use—schools, parks and playing fields, hospitals, and a great many other things, including aeroplanes, battleships, and atomic bombs. There is no way of deciding how much of such things to provide by measuring their usefulness either against their cost or against the usefulness of other things we could get for the same cost. The demand for such things is settled not by any such process of measurement, but by the judgment of Parliament, or a local authority, or some other public body or trust concerning the quantities of them it is best to have. In the making of such decisions the cost is a very relevant factor, and the total amount of them that can be supplied involves weighing one claim against others and limiting the expenditure upon them so as to take account of other uses to which the resources that would be needed to provide them could be put. But, in the last resort, such questions as ' How many schools, or how many battleships, shall we have ? ' cannot be decided except by an act of judgment that is not based on *measurement* of the value of the result.

The position is much the same when it is a question of deciding how far to carry safety precautions designed to reduce the incidence of industrial diseases or accidents, or how high a standard of factory medical and welfare services to make compulsory on business firms. The effect of enforcing improved standards in these respects may be to increase production, both by procuring better work and by reducing time lost through absences ; and these results may be to some extent measurable. What cannot be measured, but is equally relevant and important, is the effect upon the happiness and mental well-being of the men and women concerned. Someone has to decide at what point it is legitimate to regard further expenditure on these objects as involving too high a cost in relation to the results to be expected; but no such judgment can properly be made without taking account of other factors besides those which can be measured in terms of output, or those which can be measured in terms of health records, accident rates, and the like. Both these kinds of measurement are relevant; but they cannot be reduced to a common scale of quantities, and even if they could there would remain immeasurable factors which it would be necessary to take into account in forming a judgment on what should and what should not be done.

What happens in these cases is that the community as a whole, or some body authorised to speak on its behalf, either takes the place of the private consumer in bidding for the use of productive resources and thus settling how much of them to apply to this or that purpose, or compels firms to spend more than most of them would spend if they were not compelled by law. This is in principle no different from what happens in the case of ordinary consumers' demand; for the consumer performs exactly the same operation of deciding for himself (or for a household) how much of a limited income to spend on this and that, at the cost of going without other things, and is similarly under the necessity of buying certain things—e.g. clothing—which the law does not allow him to dispense with. The difference is that in the individual consumer's case the demands of many consumers are combined to form a total market demand, which is thus given an appearance of objectivity, as if it were a real measure of 'utility' in some comprehensive sense. In truth, however, a great deal of consumers' demand represents no such objective standard; for total market demand is made up of many offers which have no more in common than that they are offers of so much money for particular goods or services. Some of them may represent calculations of the usefulness of the purchase against the cost of obtaining it and against the usefulness of other things the money could buy ; but it is also true that many offers to buy have to be made without any such quantitative valuation of the thing bought. A thing may be wanted, for any of a vast variety of reasons, enough to be bought without the consumer being able to make any calculation of how much it is worth to him— only that it is worth buying. It might be so, or it might not, if more had to be paid for it : the most we can say is that it cannot be expected to be worth less than the consumer is prepared to pay—though in some cases, as in buying a house, the decision to pay the price asked may be very reluctantly reached.

Good conditions of employment, good human relations at work and elsewhere, liberty and freedom from tyranny or arbitrary power, security, participation in settling one's own conditions of work—all these may be worth buying. To the extent that they are so, men would presumably be prepared, if the choice presented itself, to accept lower incomes for work carrying such conditions than for similar work not carrying them, or carrying their opposites. This, however, it will be agreed, is a most unrealistic way of envisaging the usual conditions of wage-bargaining. Doubtless, workers are repelled from seeking employment in particular occupations or in particular works, not only by low wages, but also by bad conditions of labour or a reputation for bullying or inconsiderate management ; and, on the other hand, firms and industries can attract workers by offering good conditions and friendly management as well as by high wages. But the ability to choose the better and to reject the worse is in practice narrowly limited for most workers, even in times of full employment, by the obstacles in the way of movement out of one trade or area into another, and by the tendency for good or bad conditions to be characteristic of entire trades or areas rather than to exist side by side in establishments between which the worker is really free to choose. Under Capitalism, a particularly good firm may succeed in attracting the best workers, and a particularly bad one may have difficulty in getting the right assortment of skilled and less skilled workers when trade in general is active ; and over and above this, a rapidly expanding industry may need to offer the inducement of good conditions as well as of relatively high wages. But, except in these cases, the distribution of labour is very unresponsive to non-wage inducements, and high ' disutility ' of labour is seldom a cost that the employer is called upon to meet in full.

The socialist economist sets out, then, not with the expectation that the haggles of the labour market can be relied upon, even under full employment, to ensure that high disutility of working conditions is either paid for or eliminated, but with a determination to tackle directly the problem of ensuring that the disutility of work shall be reduced to the lowest practicable point. This involves, in the first place, insistence on high standards of accident prevention, precaution against industrial diseases, heating, lighting, ventilation, and other sanitary conditions in workplaces. The cost of such improvements has, no doubt, to be taken into the reckoning ; but the worthwhileness of a desirable measure is estimated, not exclusively or even mainly, by its *net* cost (which may be negative) after taking account of resulting improvements in output or quality of work, but also by its effects on the well-being of the workers. Limits may still have to be set to what can be afforded in the raising of standards in these respects ; but they will be set by the total limitation of the community's resources and not merely by the effects on the money or real costs of production in the establishments concerned.

In the second place, the socialist economist will insist that not only the physical conditions of work, but also the human conditions, are a matter for direct intervention in order to introduce and maintain high minimum standards. Admittedly this is a much more difficult affair to regulate by formal rules ; for men cannot be made reasonable or good-tempered by Act of Parliament. It is, however, possible to insist on the observance of certain standards of collective behaviour—on full recognition of Trade Unions, on the adoption of regular practices of ' consultation ' in the work-places by the representatives of management, on restrictions on arbitrary dismissal, and on the right of those who have to obey orders to have some say in the choice of the persons by whom the orders are to be issued. Such things are, of course, only in part matters for regulation by law : they depend largely on the strength of Trade Unionism and on the intelligence with which Trade Unionists govern their own affairs. But the State can reinforce trade union action by prescribing certain rules—e.g. by making it unlawful to refuse collective bargaining rights, by insisting, in fairly large establishments, on the maintenance of consultative machinery, by conceding rights of appeal against dismissals, and by adopting, in publicly operated industries and services, standards of ' workers ' participation ' well ahead of those to be found elsewhere.

Moreover, in relation to both physical conditions of work and human relations in industry the State can actively foster research and experiment. It can carry further the types of work already engaged in by the Industrial Health Research Board, the Institute of Industrial Psychology, the various agencies concerned with industrial hygiene and the prevention of accidents, and so on. It can, through its town-planning and housing activities, do much to improve factory lay-out and design, to build the right kinds of houses in the right places, to reduce the average length of journeys to and from work and to make them less unpleasant, to ensure adequate canteen arrangements and facilities for sport and recreation (not necessarily under works auspices), and in general to improve the amenities connected with the day's labour in both their internal and their external aspects. The State can do much, not only to make factories humanly as well as physically less unpleasant, but also to better the physical and human environment of the factory areas.

For the socialist economist all these things are as much ' Economics ' as measures designed directly to increase production. Behind them lie both the unmistakable importance of their contribution to the real achievement of a minimum standard of civilised living and also their intimate connection with the concept of democracy in its economic application. At this point, however, a further consideration enters in. It is possible for all the things that have been outlined in the foregoing paragraphs to be done in the spirit of a superior authority condescending to inferiors, without any recognition of the fundamental democratic claim that men ought to be not merely well-treated but also self-governing and in a real sense ' free and equal ' in their rights. This conception of democracy cannot fairly be denied in the economic by those who accept it in the political sphere. The socialist economist will accordingly adopt as a further maxim of economic conduct the furtherance of some sort of industrial democracy, and will reckon achievements in this field as part of the value of economic activity in a society professing democratic principles.

What does this claim amount to ? In the long run, to nothing less than that industries as much as political structure must be conducted as internally democratic concerns, dependent in the final resort on the principle of ' one man, one vote.' This idea frightens many people, because they cannot conceive of industries being efficiently run by mass-meetings. Precisely the same objection was advanced, and was widely accepted, against political democracy when it was proposed to extend voting rights to the main body of the people. But has political democracy, to the extent that it has been applied, meant that political affairs have been conducted by means of mass-meetings? Is there any likelihood that, as political democracy makes further advances, this will come to be the case? In theory no doubt, the mass of men and women, having won voting rights, could use them to insist on all decisions being made by referendum or mass-meeting, or on choosing representatives who would mirror as nearly as possible their own ignorance. But they do not. Nor do they in fact usually insist on electing by mass-vote town clerks, borough engineers, police superintendents, headmasters, civil service heads of departments, judges and magistrates, or even Cabinet Ministers. Some countries have indeed pushed the principle of direct election a good deal farther than others: the United States have been notable for the wide use of this method in their local affairs. But even in the United States the choice of responsible political officers is largely indirect; and in most parliamentary countries with a wide franchise the citizens act mainly by choosing representatives rather than executive officials. They elect members of Parliament and of a number of local authorities, and leave these elected persons to do the choosing of most of the high administrators in both local and national political affairs.

Again, some countries make use of the referendum in deciding some issues of political policy; and in this respect Switzerland, as well as the United States, has been well to the fore. But here too the more usual practice in parliamentary countries has been to leave the elected representatives of the people to carry out by legislative and executive measures the programmes with which they have appealed to the electors. In Great Britain, particularly, there has been no tendency for the extension of voting rights to bring with it any desire to adopt either the referendum or the direct election of office-holders. Such methods may be consistent with democracy : they cannot, I think, be regarded as essential parts of its application to political affairs.

Industrial or economic democracy, then, even if it rests finally on equal voting rights, does not involve the control of industrial operations by mass-meetings or referenda. What it does involve is the recognition of a claim to industrial citizenship not less far-reaching than the claim to political citizenship, but not necessarily in the same forms. The great difference is that, whereas the great majority of persons are *active* in politics only occasionally, and have little to do with its day-to-day working, those who work in industry or in some other form of productive or social service are on the job day after day, and are deeply concerned in the everyday incidents of working life. From this it follows that, whereas the requirements of political democracy can suitably be met mainly by voting arrangements leading to the choice of representatives, national and local, by the whole body of persons concerned, effective industrial democracy calls for arrangements for direct participation of the ordinary worker in the affairs of the small working unit of which he is a member—the thing closest to his daily life—even more imperatively than for a necessarily indirect share in the control of larger units. Political democracy centres round parliamentary and municipal elections : industrial democracy centres round the work-place.

I agree that, in order to make political democracy fully effective, we need to carry it below the level of Parliament and of the large local Authority and to create smaller ' neighbourhood units ' in which small groups of citizens can handle collectively such of their affairs as do not require large-scale execution. Political democracy, however, has tended in modern times to spread downwards from the national rather than upwards from the local unit. In Great Britain, Parliament advanced towards democracy faster than Local Government, which was indeed built up on more democratic lines largely by parliamentary action.[1] Industrial democracy should, on the whole, grow the opposite way, beginning mainly with the establishment of democratic rights in workshop and factory, and spreading thence to the larger units of economic control. I do not, of course, mean to lay down any exclusive rule, or to suggest that no 'workers' control' should be applied on a national or area scale until workshop democracy has become an accomplished fact. I do, however, think that it will be impracticable to find satisfactory means of democratising the higher control of industry until the practice of workshop democracy has advanced much further than it has yet.

The right foundation for democracy in industry is the general diffusion of a practice of real consultation reaching, not merely an elected shop committee or body of shop stewards, but every individual worker. It should be a part of ordinary industrial practice to take no decision that will affect any man's working life without consulting him personally before the decision is made. Even if most of the discussion takes place in a shop committee, between representatives of workers and management, the individual worker must be given a sense that his personal rights are being recognised and must be consulted directly, as well as through his representatives. This is of course largely a matter of the attitude of managers and foremen in handling workshop problems, and also to a smaller extent of the attitude of trade union and workshop representatives in consulting the 'rank and file.' *Personal* consultation

---

[1] This is less true of the United States, where the New England township had taken root before the country became an independent Republic. See de Tocqueville's *Democracy in America*.

lies at the root of the whole matter. Given that, the next thing is that workshop committees shall be, not merely 'consulted,' but also given definite, though necessarily limited, executive powers in matters of workshop concern —including, I should say, the right to veto the appointment of a foreman and perhaps to choose their own from a panel of properly qualified candidates, as well as to make collective arrangements for the distribution of jobs within the shop, the dovetailing of holidays, and similar matters which concern them much more nearly than anyone else. Of course, the workshop group cannot be allowed a final voice in matters which affect cost or quality of output. In relation to these, which affects others— indeed, the whole community—it can only claim the right to make representations, and to be listened to, when it believes it has a grievance. Such things in the last resort must be settled 'higher up', but democratic principle requires that, before they are so settled, the lesser groups affected shall be able to get their case heard, and also that in the final settlement their representatives shall be allowed a real say.

This is not the place for any full discussion of the implications of industrial democracy. My only concern at this point is to assert that socialist Economics must set out from the postulate that such democracy is a good thing, fully as much as from the postulate that higher production is a good thing, because it helps to satisfy human desires. Neither of these postulates can be pushed to an indefinite extent regardless of the other, or of further postulates which have been laid down in a previous chapter. The implications of these postulates, at some point in their application, may conflict; and then it is a matter of deciding how much weight to assign to one of them as against another. But there can, of course, be no way at all of *measuring* one kind of good against another quite different kind, so as to demonstrate which ought to be preferred. It is no more possible to measure out the *optimum* quantity of economic democracy against the potential loss of economic productivity that it may involve than there is any way of *measuring* the advantage of improved medical services against the potential productivity in other uses of the man-power needed for them.

There may, indeed, be no conflict. Better health may yield higher output, and so may economic democracy. It can be contended that men in general when they are given greater freedom and self-government in their jobs will produce more and better than under a non-democratic system of industrial management. This, however, cannot be proved either way, except by full trial over a long period ; and the whole comparison turns out, on examination, to involve many more complications than appear at first sight. For what are we to compare with what ? Most people will agree that slave labour has shown itself to be inefficient and unproductive ; yet even this is not universally the case. It is probably true even of modern timber camps as well as of Roman *latifundia* and of cotton plantations in the Southern States ; but was it true of the industrial workshops of the ancient world, where the slaves were relatively well treated ? Nobody knows. As for free, self-governing labour, there is some evidence for the view that co-operative farming in relatively primitive areas can be more productive than farming with wage-labour on large estates ; but it is not easy to be sure enough to offer a confident generalisation. In modern industry co-operative workshops seem to compete well enough with capitalist workshops where the conditions allow of efficient production in small units, and where not a great deal of capital is needed for each worker employed. They have usually failed where these conditions have not existed ; but it is not easy to say how far their failure has been due to the defects of economic democracy as a form of productive control and how far to lack of capital and other disadvantages that are external to the comparison I am trying to make.

Even if economic democracy were tried on a considerable scale, with adequate capital resources, and appeared to have adverse effects on output, this would not decide the issue ; for it is *prima facie* unlikely that men used to being controlled from above and to regarding management as an alien, if not as a hostile, force would be able to change over all of a sudden to managing their own affairs in a self-governing way without making a good many mistakes before they could get the best out of the new system. Moreover, it seems probable that there are big differences in capacity for self-government between labour groups consisting mainly of skilled workers—e.g. printers—and groups composed mainly of routine machine-minders. It also seems likely that in general women will tend to be less interested than men in workshop self-government, not because they are inferior to men, but because most of them stay less long in employment and have less chance of, or interest in, rising to responsible posts, and are mainly employed in the less skilled types of work.

When we have said all this, the main issue is still unstated. What are we comparing with what? Is it to be assumed that there is an open choice between continuing the old forms of non-self-governing employment, under the conditions that have existed hitherto, and installing institutions of industrial democracy? In a socialist, or largely socialist society, this cannot be the case. The capitalist system of employment has worked because it has been capitalist, by which I mean that it has usually been able to use the fear of the sack and of possible unemployment as an incentive to hard work and regular attendance. I do not suggest that Capitalism has relied on this incentive alone, especially in recent times ; it has more and more combined with it monetary incentives of higher piecework earnings, incentives of possible promotion to a higher grade, and attempts to promote the team spirit. It is, however, doubtful how long the capitalist form of employment can go on securing satisfactory and regular work if the fear of the sack is removed from the worker's mind, at all events to the extent of the worker feeling confident of being able easily to secure a new job corresponding to his capacity. Under conditions of full employment this is bound to be the normal situation ; but no Socialist can contemplate giving up full employment in order to be able again to crack the whip of fear at the worker as an incentive to hard work and regular atttendance. Nor, I think, can any Socialist contemplate a régime of tribunals regularly engaged in fining or otherwise disciplining slackers and absentees. Neither a return to the ' reserve of labour ' nor a new system of pains and penalties is consistent with the principles of social—let alone of industrial—democracy.

We have then to ask ourselves whether a socialist economic system can, in the long run, be made to work except on a basis of industrial self-government. Shall we not have, as the only way consistent with our democratic principles of getting hard and regular work, to place the responsibility squarely on the workers' own shoulders ? Shall we not have to do this, to a considerable extent, whether the results be higher output or not, simply because it is the only way of conducting industry that squares with socialist principles ?

CHAPTER VI

INTERNATIONAL ECONOMICS

Socialists have always been proud of being internationalists, though they have always had to work in practice mainly within national units, attempting to win power within their own countries as a step towards the establishment of fraternal relations among the peoples of the entire world. Even the Russians, in preaching world revolution, have had to try to present at any rate the appearance that each people is accomplishing its own liberation, rather than being ' forced to be free ' by the might of the Soviet Union. Where socialist parties win power by constitutional means and become the source of parliamentary governments, their first task is necessarily that of advancing towards Socialism within the national frontiers by measures of re-distribution of incomes, expansion of social services, planning for full employment, and nationalisation of such parts of the economy as seem most to need co-ordination as instruments of a planned economic policy. This necessarily involves the danger that Socialism in practice may deny its internationalist principles by becoming unduly nationalistic.

Presumably all Socialists wish to raise standards of living and to establish socialist economy over the whole world as far as this can be done. But in practice no socialist Government in a country which enjoys a relatively high standard of living can deliberately set out to reduce that standard in order to raise standards elsewhere. The British workers, however socialist they might be in sentiment, would not consent to their standards being reduced in order to improve the standards of Africans or Malayans or West Indians—to say nothing of East Indians or Chinese. Democracy, even socialist democracy, cannot be expected to exercise altruism to such an extent. The most that can be looked for is that a socialist country will not set out to enrich itself further at the expense of others, and will do its best to help the advancement of other peoples wherever this can be done without sacrifices of actual welfare among its own people.

Socialism is not a guaranteed cure for human selfishness; but it can reasonably be expected that the establishment of more co-operative relations between man and man within a socialist community will be reflected in an improved morality in international dealings. This qualified assumption is the basis on which it seems reasonable to approach the study of socialist Economics in its international aspects.

International Economics centre round two closely connected groups of questions—those relating to the international exchange of goods and services and those relating to money, where payments need to be made across national frontiers. These are, indeed, really two aspects of one and the same problem; for money comes in as an international factor because of the need to organise payment for goods and services passing in international exchange. The trading aspect must evidently be considered first; for it is the real substance, whereas money is only a means towards real exchanges of goods and services. Money can even be dispensed with altogether where direct barter of goods can be arranged. But barter has great inconveniences as a normal way of trading, though it has its uses in exceptional cases as a stimulus to trade that would not otherwise exist.

The socialist economist sets out from the assumption that the broad lines of foreign trade will be planned, at any rate at the national level, wherever Socialism exists. The purpose of this planning will be (1) to ensure adequate imports of things which either cannot be produced at home or can be produced in sufficient quantities only at unduly high real costs. This involves that, in one way or another, the importing country shall be able to pay for these things, and, in the main, this can be done only by exporting goods and services acceptable as fair equivalents for the imports required. A further purpose will be (2) to make arrangements with other countries whereby specialisation in production can be fostered to the mutual advantage of the countries concerned, so as to decrease the real cost of producing the goods and services that are wanted in all these countries, regarded as forming a complementary group of consumers. The first of these purposes involves national planning of imports and exports of goods and services ; the second involves some degree of concerted international planning. The difference between Socialists and the old *laissez-faire* economists is so far one, not of objective, but of method. The Socialist believes that the best way to bring about useful economic specialisation is to plan for it, not to wait for it to happen of itself, under conditions which may set up all sorts of awkward reactions on the balance of payments and on the structure of the national economy, and may thus lead to restrictionist measures in an attempt to cope with these reactions. On this issue, many modern non-socialist economists are prepared to go a long way with the Socialists—though not all the way.

The desirability of international trade for procuring things, such as particular materials or foodstuffs, which simply cannot be got at home needs no demonstration. It is also plain that the requisite trade in such things could not proceed unless there were also trade in other things ; for there can be no assurance that a country will be able to pay for its imports of such things with exports of which other countries stand in the same absolute need. Raw materials and the climatic conditions required for growing crops or nurturing livestock are not so distributed over the earth as to establish a natural balance of such exchanges; nor is there, except in the case of minerals, any permanent and absolute law determining what each country can produce. In every area the conditions permanently rule out some kinds of production; but there remains a wide range over which what can be produced at any period depends on historical rather than on sheerly natural causes. The very root of international trading may rest on the natural differentiation of regions; the tree which springs from that root has many branches which have been grafted upon it by the historical development of the various societies of mankind.

A socialist country, then, will, perforce or voluntarily, import many things which it is not absolutely prevented from producing at home, or from doing without by the use of tolerable home-made substitutes, and will export many things which the recipients could, if they were put to it, make for themselves or similarly do without. What, then, will guide the planners in such a society in framing their international trading policy? Largely, no doubt, they will be following a traditional pattern which neither they nor anyone else can fully explain; but what interests us is not the pattern itself so much as the changes in it which are made from time to time. What, we need to ask, will guide the planners in making changes either in what they decide to import or in what they seek to sell to their neighbours? Unless they have resources available from what is owing to them on account of past unrequited exports of goods or services, or are enabled to receive unrequited imports by way of loan or gift, they will have to aim at exporting the full equivalent of what they import. Indeed, they will have to succeed in this, for, subject to the exceptions mentioned, they will not get more imports than they can pay for. There will have to be an overall balance—not a balance, bilaterally, with any particular country from which imports are desired, but an overall balance on the total trading account including payments for services, such as shipping, as well as for goods.

According to the classical doctrine, the nature and volume of international trade are determined, in the absence of artificial hindrances, such as tariffs, quotas and licensing systems, by considerations of 'comparative cost.' Under conditions of complete free trade between buyers and sellers over all the world each country will produce such things, and such quantities of them, as will make possible the highest total world production at the lowest cost. This does not mean that, at any moment, everything will be produced where it costs least to produce it; for resources of capital and labour are not completely fluid at short notice between place and place, and in practice the need for each country to balance its overall receipts and payments will mean that some countries will have to produce things that could be made at less cost elsewhere in order to pay for imports they badly need. But a country which is under this necessity will have to exchange what it produces at a comparative disadvantage for things that have been produced at lower *real* cost elsewhere. It will have to put up with a lower return than corresponds to its costs in terms of the resources used up in production—in other words, with a lower standard of living than would accrue to its citizens if the diversity of its productive resources allowed it to concentrate only on producing what it can produce at as low a cost as any other country. In the classical theory such disparities will always be tending to disappear, because both capital and human beings will tend to migrate to the areas in which they can be most productively employed. But in practice, as most modern economists, whatever their politics, agree, such migration cannot always occur; and, even where it can, it is bound to take time, as it took time to fill America with emigrants from

Europe before restrictions had been imposed on their entry.

The classical theory of the international division of labour obviously contains a substantial element of truth, as describing what happens when capital and labour move freely across national frontiers in pursuit of economic advantage. To the extent to which they cannot or will not move, the theory still has much truth ; but it involves not that everything will tend to be produced wherever it can be produced at the lowest cost, so as to maximise total world wealth, but only that countries will tend, in the absence of restrictions on imports and exports, to produce those things in which they are either at the greatest comparative advantage in cost or at the least comparative disadvantage. A country which could produce at lower cost than others more than enough things to occupy all its capital and labour will tend to pick and choose those forms of production in which its advantage is greatest, and to leave other countries to produce for it things in which its comparative advantage is less, as well as those in which it is at a comparative disadvantage. Countries less favourably situated will have to produce things for which they are at a disadvantage, but will pick those in which their disadvantage is least for export to their more fortunate neighbours. The extent of comparative advantages and disadvantages will appear in the relative standards of living of the various countries, as measured by their national incomes *per caput*.

This is all very well up to a point ; but the classical economists were led by their appreciation of the virtues of national specialisation as a foundation for international trade to the false notion that international trade was an unqualified good, and that the volume of commodities passing in international exchanges furnished the best measure of economic progress. Looking at the question from the standpoint of the most advanced countries, which had the lowest real costs of production for a wide range of manufactured goods, they ignored the possibility that Free Trade might, in giving the capitalists of these countries the pick of the world market, condemn countries that were behindhand in economic techniques to remain permanently undeveloped, because they could not hope to produce in competition with the more advanced countries either without the aid of capital borrowed from such countries or, even with such aid, until they had been through a period of relatively high-cost production while they were learning the new techniques. This omission did not escape the notice of such economists as Friedrich List, the father of modern protectionism, who held Free Trade to be the advantage of the countries that were already in the van of efficiency, but to the detriment of those which were capable of catching up, but had not yet developed their productive powers. Therewith, List argued that many countries were incapable, even in the long run, of acclimatising the higher industrial techniques, and should be content to develop their agricultural and extractive industries for the exchange of their products for manufactured goods from the more advanced countries.

This view, though it was rejected by the orthodox classical schools, seemed plausible at the time it was expressed (in the 1840s), and had a great influence in both the United States and Germany. It is more influential than ever to-day, but with a marked change of emphasis, in that many countries which List regarded as doomed to serve merely as suppliers of foodstuffs and materials for their more fortunate neighbours are no longer prepared to accept this position, and see no reason why they should not be able to develop industries of their own or why, even if such industries must operate for a time at high real costs, their existence is to be regarded as not worth while. In effect, as soon as there appears any limit to the amounts of foodstuffs and materials that can be sold abroad, or any tendency for the prices of such exports to decline in relation to other prices, the less advanced countries, unable to buy from the more advanced the supplies of manufactured goods which they need, may do better to produce manufactures for themselves at a higher real cost, rather than go without them. They are thus induced both by the hope of joining the ranks of the advanced countries and by their own unsatisfied needs to embark on the development of their own industries, and to resort to protectionist measures in order to uphold their own products in their home markets.

It cannot reasonably be argued that such a policy is wrong, though it is very often pursued in a wrong way, by producing the wrong things, by enabling the home manufacturers to reap undue profits, and by diffusing protection over too wide a field and thus encouraging scattered home production instead of concentrating effort on a few things and thus making it easier to attain to tolerable efficiency. Nor can it be reasonably held, as it was by the classical economists, that a high level of foreign trade is necessarily a sign of economic progress; for, as more countries become adepts in up-to-date manufacturing techniques, it inevitably happens that a number of them develop the same kinds of aptitude and that differences of efficiency between firms in a country come to be larger in many cases than differences between whole industries in different countries. As this happens, it ceases to be realistic to think of each country as having its own level of productivity for a particular type of goods, so as to be suitable or unsuitable for carrying on a particular industry. The advantages of international specialisation do not of course disappear; but their range tends to become relatively narrower, and it may be more advantageous to devote attention to raising the efficiency of the less productive units within a country over a wide range than to develop an exclusive specialisation within a narrower field. In other words, whereas the earlier classical economists thought in terms of unorganised competition between firms, regardless of frontiers, and at the same time assumed that the *aggregate* of firms in one country would be more productive than the competing aggregate in another, the modern economist has become aware of the logical fallacy involved in this way of thinking, and has come either to disregard *national* differences altogether and to argue entirely in terms of competition between *firms*, wherever situated, or, alternatively, to recognise *national* differences, but therewith to think more in terms of national combination and rationalisation of production and not of competing *firms*.

Thus, modern non-socialist economists have moved a long way from the ideas of the classical schools, and Free Trade is no more in theory than in practice the sacred dogma it once was for Great Britain. Even apart from the influence of ideas of planning, sheer circumstances have forced modern economists to think more on national lines, because they can no longer take for granted that the balance of trade will look after itself. Trying to regulate the balance of payments by controlling imports and stimulating exports involves at least a rudimentary planning of the pattern of foreign trade. But underneath this unavoidable preoccupation with the problems of balance, most modern economists still keep a belief in the virtue of the old classical doctrine, as showing how things *ought to* work out, even if in this imperfect world they cannot conform to the proper economic rules.

How far will socialist foreign trade reproduce this pattern? In capitalist societies it has never existed in any complete form, for resources of capital and manpower have never been fluid to more than a limited extent; and over and above this the pattern of trade has usually been distorted by all manner of protective devices for fostering particular branches of production, either because they have powerful vested interests behind them, or for reasons of national security or prestige, or in order to protect balances of payments against an excess of imports. In the first place, it is clearly advantageous for a society, whatever its economic system may be, to employ its resources in producing whatever things it needs and can produce at home with less cost and effort than would be involved in producing exports to exchange for them. The limits to this are set, first, by the available supply of resources for producing the things in question (which of course are different in the long and in the short run), and secondly by the quantities of such goods that are needed more than other things that could be produced, or exchanged for exports produced, with the same expenditure of resources.

Even this elementary principle is, however, in practice a good deal less simple than it appears ; for production has to be arranged for in advance, and the relative costs of producing things at home and getting them from abroad do not remain constant over time. Accordingly, decisions about home production have to be based on estimates of future cost relations, and these estimates may turn out wrong even if they are made as carefully as possible. This is the case especially with agricultural production, in face both of uncertain crop yields and of the special influences affecting the prices of foodstuffs in the world market ; but it applies also to other classes of goods, the cost of which may be affected by economic fluctuations, currency changes, or speculative influences. Of course, all these factors operate in capitalist economies, and capitalist business men, as well as government planners, have to base their reckonings of what is worth while to produce on anticipations about future cost relations. Public planning, however, transfers the main responsibility for estimating from private *entrepreneurs* to the public authority responsible for the plan ; and this is likely to mean in practice that in the case of standard goods that can be bought in bulk there will be some form of collective purchasing, based wherever possible on long-term contracts designed to check speculative price movements and to ensure steady supplies of required imports by assuring overseas producers of a continuing market.

There has been much controversy about the effects of such bulk buying, as against those of 'free market' buying. On the one hand it is argued that either competitive private buyers or a public buying agency not tied down by long-term contracts will be able to buy goods most cheaply by taking full advantage of periods of low prices to build up stocks and by refraining from buying when prices are high. This argument assumes that what is wanted is the lowest possible price, rather than a price fair to buyer and seller alike. It also appears to assume that the buyer or buyers concerned are in a better bargaining position than other people; for clearly sellers will wish to behave in a precisely opposite way. On the other side is the argument that long-term contracts actually reduce production costs by enabling producers to plan for a known market, and that fair prices mutually arranged form a much firmer foundation for stable trading relationships and for improved standards of security than can be got by attempting to snatch unfair advantages. We shall have to return to this point when we come to consider the international, as distinct from the purely national, planning of foreign trade.

So far, we have noted that no occasion for imports will ordinarily arise when a country can produce as much as it needs of a thing at less cost than it would incur in producing exports that could be exchanged for the quantity required. But, of course, a country which is in this position will commonly be able to go on and produce additional supplies of the same commodity for sale abroad at prices which other countries will be prepared to pay. The cost of producing such additional supplies will be the marginal cost, *i.e.* the difference between the cost of producing the quantity needed at home and the cost of producing any larger supply. This marginal cost may be less, equal to, or more than the cost per unit of supplies for the home market. It will be desirable to carry production to the point at which marginal cost looks like being about equal to the selling price in the world market, or, in other words, the point at which it would become necessary to consider whether it might not be better to use any further available resources of capital (including land) and labour in producing something else.

Where a country can produce a part, but not the whole, of its requirements of a commodity at a lower real cost than would be involved in producing exports to exchange for it, a socialist economy will normally produce up to this point, and will import the balance of what it needs. But in framing its estimates of needs for the various kinds of goods it will have to keep its total purchases from abroad within the limits set by the willingness of other countries to receive its exports. This is, of course, in part a matter of the prices charged ; but it is not wholly so, for other countries will also need to keep total imports down to what they can pay for, and may be restricting imports in order to protect certain of their own industries against foreign competition. Where protective policies are in force, there may be absolute obstacles to any increase in sales through offering goods at a lower price ; but where imports are restricted only in order to preserve the balance of payments the assurance of an enlarged market for a country's exports will make it ready to receive additional imports. This has been the basis, in recent years, for many bilateral trade bargains, providing for planned increases in exchanges between pairs of countries, to the benefit of both. It is, however, usually difficult to advance very far by planning bilateral exchanges of goods for goods, because where it is a question of exchanging certain quantities of primary products—foodstuffs or materials—for manufactured goods the diversity of the latter makes it difficult, if not impossible, to specify the precise goods that are to be exchanged. Accordingly, what commonly happens is that the bulk purchase of certain quantities of primary products is matched by the opening of an equivalent money credit which can be spent by any exporting country on any of the products, or any of a wide range of products, of the importing country. Sometimes there is no bulk purchase of any particular goods on either side, but each of the pair of countries opens a credit in favour of the other, to be spent on its products, so that every purchase opens the way to an offsetting sale.

Objection is often taken to these kinds of bilateral transaction on the ground that they tend to force international trade into an artificial pattern of bilateral balancing, whereas the ideal of 'free' intercourse requires that every country (or rather each business in every country) shall be able to buy and sell where it pleases without any 'discrimination.' There is clearly no need for each country to balance its trade with each other, if each can secure an overall balance by exporting in the aggregate as much as it imports—provided that *each* country does in fact secure such a balance. If Country A buys more from Country B than Country B buys from Country A, this does not matter if over the same period Country A sells more to Country C than it buys from Country C, and Country C balances the account by selling more to Country B than it buys from Country B. Such three-cornered trade is of course very common— for example, Great Britain meets part of the cost of its imports from the United States out of the proceeds of Malayan rubber and tin which are paid for by British exports to Malaya or by claims due to British investors in Malayan industries. This multilateral balancing may of course take very much more complicated forms, involving not three, but many, countries. It works out as long as *each* country overall imports and exports the relative quantities of goods and services needed to balance its international accounts. If, however, any one country exports *more* than it needs to export in order to cover the cost of its imports, it follows that some other country or countries must be failing to achieve a balance ; and when that happens, unless the 'surplus' country fills the gap with loans or gifts, the 'deficit' country or countries must reduce imports to the level required to establish a balance.

In what has been said so far, I have left out the complications that arise from the existence in each country of a separate currency of its own. Each seller normally wants in the last resort to be able to get paid in the money of his own country. Where any national money can be freely exchanged for any other at a fixed price and in unlimited amount this result is secured ; but such exchange can be assured only when the demand for each kind of money is in balance with the supply, and that means, in effect, where each country's balance of payments is in equilibrium. Every exchange of one kind of money for another is a two-way transaction. Every demand for dollars means that someone must be prepared to part with dollars in exchange for some other kind of money, or the demand cannot be met. But where trade does not balance, so that the total demand for, say, dollars exceeds the total supply, one of two things is bound to occur. If there is no fixed rate of exchange between the different national currencies, a currency which is scarce in relation to the demand will rise in value in terms of other currencies until a balance is restored by the fall in the international purchasing power of the currencies which are in excess supply. Where, on the other hand, relative currency values are fixed, as they must be where each currency is exchangeable for a fixed amount of gold, the countries which find themselves in deficit on their balance of payments will be forced to restrict by direct measures of control their imports from the countries whose currencies are scarce. In either case, the deficit countries will be driven to limit their purchases from the surplus countries to what they can afford to pay for, either out of the proceeds of exports or by sending gold, if they have any, to the surplus countries in payment for imports.

When a country, or a group of countries, finds itself in this situation in relation to a surplus country or group of countries, the only alternative to a reduction of imports is a diversion of trade to countries of which the currencies are or can be made less scarce. Thus, during the past few years Great Britain and other deficit areas have been forced to seek to replace supplies which have to be paid for in dollars by supplies from other sources—for example, in the sterling area or in continental Europe. This, however, can be done only to the extent to which the alternative suppliers are prepared to receive payment in additional exports from the countries needing their products; and this usually involves the making of bilateral bargains, or sometimes of limited multilateral bargains among a group of countries for the mutual exchange of their products. It is inconsistent with full multilateralism, whereby all sums received from the sale of exports can be spent anywhere in the world. Such multilateralism is practicable only when every country is prepared to receive imports on a scale sufficient to enable all the purchasers of its products to meet without limit the claims due to it from the rest of the world.

Under present conditions, a socialist country, equally with countries working under a capitalist system, must find itself under the necessity of restricting its dollar purchases to what it can pay for out of the proceeds of its exports to dollar countries, or out of loans or gifts made to it by such countries—*e.g.* under ' Marshall Aid.' The difference between a socialist and a capitalist country finding itself in this predicament is that, whereas the latter, broadly speaking, can limit its imports only by imposing restrictions through tariffs or prohibitions on particular imports, or by restricting the total supply of dollar exchange available to importing firms, a socialist country can in addition strike direct bargains for the bulk import of supplies from non-dollar sources in exchange for its own manufactures, and can thus endeavour to decrease its long-run dependence on supplies from dollar areas by building up trading relations elsewhere. Of course, a capitalist country can do the same thing, if it is prepared to resort to ' state trading ', but that is only to say that capitalist countries can use socialist methods, as becomes plainly evident in time of war.

Such a policy, to which Great Britain and other countries were driven by the scarcity of dollars, met at the outset with strong objections from the United States on the ground that it involved ' discrimination ' and thus violated the principles of ' free, multilateral trading.' It was, however, impracticable for the Americans to sustain their objections, in face of the sheer inability of other countries to find the means of paying for all the imports they wanted from the United States. Even when it had been agreed to grant ' Marshall Aid ' on a large scale to the deficit countries, the need to keep this aid within limits forced the United States not merely to acquiesce in the aided countries' search for alternative sources of supply, but actually to encourage this search as a necessary means of restoring balance to the trading relations of these countries. The Americans continued to proclaim their theoretical objections to bilateral, discriminative trading arrangements, and to look forward to a future in which they would be no longer needed; but in practice they had to recognise the unavoidableness of bilateral or, at the least, limited bargains for as long as countries could not hope, without it, to balance their international accounts.

From the socialist standpoint, there is everything to be said for bilateral or limited multilateral bargains, where they can be made between countries in such a way as to enlarge the volume of exchanges on mutually advantageous terms—for example, by stimulating the increased production of needed primary products in mainly agricultural countries in exchange for supplies of capital goods required for the development of productive efficiency in such countries. It is, however, highly undesirable, from the socialist as well as from any other reasonable standpoint, to carry bilateralism to the point at which the total exchanges between pairs of countries are required to balance; for clearly this cannot be done without forfeiting many of the advantages of specialisation and economic international division of labour. Accordingly, where full multilateralism is impracticable, it is advantageous to seize every opportunity that offers for multilateralism of a more limited kind; and this can best be brought about by concerted international planning among groups of countries—for example, in Western Europe, or in the Commonwealth—and by agreements between groups of countries for the exchange of complementary products—*e.g.* between Western and Eastern Europe as complementary regional groups.

In 1948-49 the 'Marshall Aid' countries all submitted to the United States separate national plans setting forth their anticipated needs for American help in the light of their expectations of their several abilities to meet their own needs either out of their home production or by exchanging their products for those of other countries. Each of these national plans inevitably involved assumptions about what the other countries concerned were expected to produce either for home consumption or for export; and it immediately appeared that the plans were inconsistent in many respects, because they involved irreconcilable assumptions about the exports of particular kinds of goods which the world market could be expected to absorb. It therefore became necessary for the 'Marshall Aid' countries to endeavour to harmonise their several plans by reaching some agreement about the quantities of the various goods which they were to set out to produce either for home consumption or for export to one another or to the rest of the world; and, as I write, this process of mutual modification of the initial plans is going on in a series of difficult negotiations between the countries concerned.

The difficulties in the way of such concerted planning would inevitably be great, in face of the strength of economic nationalism, even if each country were socialistic enough to have an effective control over the productive activities of its own industries and over the development of its foreign trade. The difficulties are very much the greater because, in most of the countries affected, no such controlling power exists to an adequate extent. A socialist country, in a position to plan its own production and to determine what exports to offer for sale and what imports to buy with the proceeds, is obviously in a much better position than a capitalist country to enter into mutual planning arrangements with its neighbours, both for the exchange of its exports for the imports it requires and for the agreed allocation of certain kinds of production so as to make possible the economies of large-scale output for a wide and assured market. There are limits to what can be achieved in both these respects where a socialist country has to strike mutual bargains with countries that are not socialist, or prepared to adopt socialist methods; and these limits are narrower where it is a question of planning for the international specialisation of manufacturing production than where it is mainly one of bulk purchases of primary products in exchange for exports of manufactured goods.

Socialists look forward to a world trade system which will rest on multilateral foundations, in that it will not be based on any attempt to arrive at balanced exchanges of goods and services between pairs of countries. But they seek this multilateral trading system *through planning* —both national planning of production and of foreign trade, and supranational planning among groups of countries designed to promote co-operation, instead of competition, in meeting the consumers' needs. With this end in view, they believe in bulk purchase of primary products, in order to give producers the assurance of a steady market, and in planned arrangements for the supply of exports, expecially of capital goods for the development of productivity in the less advanced countries in exchange for these primary products. They believe, too, in the concerted supranational planning of production in respect both of the agricultural and extractive industries and of manufacturing, in order to encourage specialisation and thus further the economies of large-scale production in countries whose home markets are too small to render it practicable without assured outlets for exports.

In all this, the assumptions of socialist economics are by no means wholly unlike the classical theory of the international division of labour. But, whereas the classical theory in its pure form assumed the complete fluidity of the factors of production across national frontiers, the socialist economist sets out from no such unreal premise, even in a qualified form, but begins by assuming that each country, or group of co-operating countries, will be organising its economic affairs in such a way as to provide full employment for its man-power, and will be seeking to arrange its international trade in such a way as to harmonise with this primary objective. Of course, this is not meant to exclude *voluntary* migration across national frontiers, but it is meant to exclude enforced emigration owing to the inability to find employment at home. A man's right to find maintenance in return for labour in his own country is one of the human rights which Socialists unequivocally affirm ; and from this it follows that the socialist conception of international trade is subject to the condition of full employment as a primary objective of national policy.

CHAPTER VII

SOCIALIST ECONOMIC VALUES

I HAVE so far said nothing at all in this book about Marxism, for the simple reason that I have found nothing relevant to say. Had I been writing, not a statement of socialist Economics, but a critique of Capitalism, I should have found in Marx's writings a great deal to cite with strong agreement, as well as some things to criticise in my turn. But Marx neither wrote nor ever set out to write the Economics of Socialism—an attempt which he would have regarded in his day as altogether premature. His chief book—*Capital*—was an exposure of the working of Capitalism as a system of economic exploitation which he regarded as destined to break down on account of its inherent 'contradictions,' and in it he made no attempt to show how the alternative system of Socialism would actually operate. Nor in his other writings did he ever essay such a demonstration. He simply pointed to a future in which, class-antagonisms having been finally resolved, men and peoples would work together under conditions of full 'co-operation,' and all exploitation would cease. He did, indeed, in his *Critique of the Gotha Programme of the German Social Democratic Party* say something about the principles of distribution of incomes that he expected to prevail in the transitional period from Capitalism to Socialism; but this was only to assert that the correct principle for this period would be to abolish unearned incomes and to distribute earned incomes in proportion to services rendered, without any precise indication of the means of assessing services. For the rest, Marx was at all times much more a sociologist and social historian than an economist in the ordinary sense of the term. He built his entire *corpus* of doctrine round the Materialist Conception of History, and made his detailed study of the working of capitalist society in the light of this conception and as a revelation of the historic tendency of capitalist production. Thinking always in terms of a social revolution that would in due course violently overthrow Capitalism and put the dictatorship of the proletariat in its place as the controlling force in society, he did not concern himself at all with what would happen should there be no such revolution and no such dictatorship, but instead a gradual development of Socialism through the democratic conquest of the existing State. Except in a few passages, on which it would be unwise to put undue emphasis, he denied that such a change could come about, even in Great Britain or the United States; for, regarding the State as essentially the political expression of the domination of a particular economic class, he could not envisage its conquest and utilisation by the exploited classes, but only its overthrow and replacement by a brand-new State made in the image of the new class rulers—the proletariat.

Superficially, no doubt, Marx appears to have written a great deal about Economics, putting forward a theory of value radically different from that of the classical economists whom he attacked, and therewith a theory of ' surplus value ' that cast the doctrine of class-exploitation into a form based on his restatement of the classical economic dogmas. In all this, however, Marx was in fact engaging in a dialectical argument with the Ricardians about what really followed from their own fundamental assumptions. He was seeking to demonstrate that the capitalist system rested upon a robbery of the propertyless classes; and he was not discussing at all how things would work out if ' the expropriators were expropriated ' and the common man were able to enter into his inheritance. Classical Economics set out to be mainly a discussion of the forces determining *prices*, including not only the prices of things, but also the price of human labour. Marx, having shown that the price of labour-power was always less than the value of the product of labour because the owners of the means of production always took a share of the labourer's product for themselves, was but little interested in the mechanisms which actually determined the market prices of the various kinds of commodities—including labour power. So little was he concerned that no account of the working of these mechanisms under Capitalism appears until we get to the third (posthumous) volume of *Capital* ; and when we do get to this subject we find that what Marx has to say about it differs little in essentials from what John Stuart Mill had said before him.

There is, then, nothing in Marx's writings that has any important bearing on the matters discussed in this book. There is nothing that throws any light, save in the most general terms, on the principles to be followed in distributing scarce resources among alternative uses, on the desirable levels of consumption and capital accumulation in a socialist society, on the methods to be used in assessing the remuneration of the various kinds of producers or in deciding between ' free,' collective provision of services and leaving the consumers to exercise their own choice on the desirable allocation of time between work and leisure—or, in effect, about any of the questions which I have here dealt with because they seem to me the vital issues of socialist economic construction. To say this does not mean that I accept, instead of Marxism, the assumptions and values of capitalist Economics : indeed, I have made it abundantly plain that I do not. It means that Marxism and the kind of socialist Economics that is relevant to the constructive problems of a socialist society are on quite different planes.[1]

[1] For a further discussion of this difference of plane see the chapters dealing with 'The Theory of Value' in my book, *The Meaning of Marxism* (1948).

Does this, it may be asked, involve a denial that socialist Economics call for any distinctive theory of value? I think it does, if by such a theory of value is meant anything more than a theory of market prices stripped of its expression in terms of any particular currency. I can see no *economic* use for a theory of value which, like Marx's, fails to throw any light at all on the factors affecting the relative prices of different kinds of goods—though, of course, such a theory may, and in Marx does, serve as an instrument for expounding a more general theory of the exploitation of the propertyless class. The strength of Marx's theory of value lies not in the account of how values are determined under the conditions of pure Capitalism, but in its use as a basis for the theory of 'surplus value.' But even in this aspect it is formally outmoded; for Marx took over from the Ricardians a theory of value which no one in the modern world accepts, and the theory of 'surplus value' can be much better expounded directly as a theory of monopolistic exploitation without bringing in any of the complications of the Ricardian doctrine.

Thus, the socialist economist of to-day begins by asserting that private property in the means of production is essentially of a monopolistic character, and constitutes an artificial monopoly, protected by law, which enables the property owner to levy tribute upon the fruits of other men's labours. The property-owning monopolist thus tends, as Marx pointed out, to appropriate to himself the benefits of the increasingly 'co-operative' character of the productive process, which more and more prevents the individual worker from having either an identifiable product of his own or any access to the means of production, without the owners' leave, or to the market. This position of monopoly—or, as Mr. H. D. Dickinson has termed it, 'institutional revenue'[1]—enables the owners of capital

---

[1] See H. D. Dickinson, *Institutional Revenue*.

to exploit those who have only their labour-power to offer for sale; and what Marx called 'surplus value' is in effect identical with the institutional revenues accruing to the owners of the means of production.

No doubt others besides capitalists can appropriate 'institutional revenues.' Trade Unionism, in one of its aspects, is a form of monopoly aiming at the raising of wages, for narrower or wider bodies of workers, above the point to which they would be forced down if the workers did not combine. Given a condition of full employment, and a will to take advantage of it, the Trade Unions could be powerful monopolists; indeed, no one can know the limits of their economic power, because its full exercise is always in practice restrained by a number of factors—by State-enforced arbitration, by fears of the effects on employment and production, and by a tendency for one Union to keep fairly well in step with another, in accordance with conceptions of fair wage relativities. The question is whether Trade Union monopoly is of the same kind with capitalist or landlord monopoly, or of a different order. It seems to me to be of a different order because what the labourer has to sell is his own labour, not a piece of property that could function just as well without him. *All* the return a capitalist or a landlord gets on his property is institutional monopoly revenue, because it all depends on the legal institution of private property. The labourer, on the other hand, cannot work without consuming: he must put into himself the energy which he expends on work. Accordingly, what he gets becomes an institutional monopoly revenue only if it exceeds the value of what he produces.

Socialism postulates as its aim the socialisation of all institutional monopoly revenues, except those which it will abolish altogether, such as the revenues arising from monopolistic restriction as a means to excessive prices and profits, and any parallel revenues accruing to particular kinds of labour (including that of highly paid professionals) from the same cause. Institutional monopoly revenue derived from mere property ownership it will set out to socialise, however much its exponents may be prepared to temper the wind to the shorn capitalist during a reasonable period of transition. To the extent to which these property revenues are done away with, or transferred to the public, it becomes possible to put the distribution of incomes on a fairer basis and to approach equality as nearly as can be made consistent with the need for monetary incentives to high production and with the sense of the people about what is fair as between man and man and between one occupation and another. I have made it clear in previous chapters that I know of no magic formula whereby fairness in these matters can be measured, except that there is always a strong presumption in favour of the nearest approach to sheer equality that is compatible with high output and with public sentiment.

As for a theory of value in relation to commodities, as distinct from labour-power, what is the use of it? A pricing system there must be in any society that is not rich enough to allow everyone to have as much as he wants of *everything*—unless indeed *everything* is to be rationed out irrespective of differing personal wants and desires. In any sensibly organised society, for as far ahead as it is profitable to attempt to look, a great many things will be 'rationed' by prices, so as to allow consumers to choose freely between alternative goods. Accordingly a socialist society will have to establish rules for pricing goods and services, and will presumably price them somehow according to their relative costs of production, except where there are valid social reasons for either reducing the price by subsidy or raising it by taxation in order to encourage or discourage particular kinds of consumption. It will, however, as we have seen in previous chapters, no longer be possible to regard costs as throughout objectively determined by the higgling of the market; for they will include elements which will be in the last resort subject to collective social control. The rent of land, the interest to be charged for the use of capital locked up in production, will have to be determined by the collective agencies entrusted with these functions, and the sums charged will accrue to these agencies as trustees for the public. Similarly, wages and other incomes paid in return for productive service will not be left to be settled in the last resort by the relative economic power of the various groups of workers and of the public agencies which employ them. They will have to be planned in accordance with notions of social justice and expediency, and not fought over in industrial conflict or settled exclusively by the forces of supply and demand.

Costs, therefore, will be affected by collective decisions about rent, interest on capital, and remuneration of services of different types, and the prices which correspond to costs of production will be the resultants of these decisions. But prices so determined, no less than prices settled in any other way, will accurately reflect the real costs of production in terms of the resources and the effort used up in providing each commodity, in accordance with the relative valuations set by the society on the services performed by the various factors. Prices thus established will confront the consumers as objective facts, to which they will be able to adjust their purchases so as to extract as much satisfaction as they know how out of their limited incomes. Moreover, consumers' choice, acting freely in relation to this objective price-structure, will be able to exert its influence on supply; for the planning of production will be continually reacting to consumers' behaviour by expanding the supply of goods for which there is an active demand, and reducing supplies of things that the consumers appear to want less of. The planners, moreover, will be in as good a position as possible both for estimating the probable effects on demand of raising or lowering particular prices and for working out the effects on unit costs of expanding or contracting the output of particular things. No 'theory of value' can give any help towards the making of wise judgments in such matters; all that is needed is adequate statistical information and tolerable common sense.

To some of my readers this may be a disappointing conclusion; for some of them may feel that socialist Economics ought to differ much more momentously from capitalist Economics than I have made out. But surely it will be agreed, by those who reflect, that the differences go deep enough. The essential difference indeed lies in the socialist refusal to accept the view that labour is a commodity, to be priced in the market like any other at what it will fetch. This doctrine is in fact tenable only on the assumption, which non-socialist economists often tacitly make, of a reserve of labour unable to obtain regular employment; for where conditions of full employment exist, and are guaranteed as a matter of public policy, the possibility of settling wage-rates by the 'law of the market' is in practice no longer open. Instead of a number of employers bargaining for labour against a much larger number of workers, in a situation which loads the dice against the workers because of their lesser power of endurance, there arises a situation in which nationally owned or controlled industries and services have to bargain with Trade Unions possessing a monopoly of most kinds of skilled labour, in circumstances which no longer allow the threat of starvation to be held over the worker's head, except by the deliberate action of the State. Under such conditions, though bargaining may continue as the normal method of adjusting wage-rates, there is bound to be in the background some sort of collective determination of what is deemed to be fair. A situation in which the total sum available for paying out as income and the prices to be charged for the various kinds of goods and services are alike subject to control by a general planning authority cannot leave wages uncontrolled ; for, if the total to be paid out is fixed, one group can get more only at the expense of others.

As long as human productive power continues to fall short of what is needed to satisfy all human desires for the products of human effort, some pricing of goods and services will be the best way of safeguarding individual freedom to choose between alternative forms of satisfaction. But the price system of a socialist economy will rest, not on the arbitrariness of the market, but on a structure of costs embodying socially determined valuations of the rewards due to the various producers and also of the charges to be made for the use of land and capital employed in production. The making of these valuations will be a task of social judgment—the more, not the less, valid because it will exclude, on the one hand, the exploitation of the producers by private owners of the means of production and, on the other, the treatment of human labour as a commodity to be priced as if it were a sack of potatoes or a yard of cloth. Socialist Economics are human Economics, taking as their foundation the human claims of individuals as producers and as consumers and not the alleged 'law' of a market dominated by the private appropriation of the means to human welfare.

INDEX

ABSTINENCE, 14 f., 16, 18, 25
Accidents, prevention of, 112, 113
American Revolution, 29
Arbitration, 146
Aristocracy, claims of, 11
Artists, 56
Australia, wage policy in, 68

BALANCE OF PAYMENTS, 63, 71, 72 ff., 123, 124 ff., 130, 133 ff.
Barter, 123
Bentham, Jeremy, 28
Beveridge, Lord, 78
Bilateralism. *See* Trade Agreements.
Blanc, Louis, 37
Boards, Public industrial, 54
Booms and slumps, 27, 54
Budget deficits, 46
Bulk purchase, 72, 132, 134, 140

CALCULATION, economic, 7 f. *See also* Measurability.
Canteens, industrial, 114

Capital, accumulation of, 15, 19, 22, 38, 64, 144
  as cost of production, 16, 20
  finance, 20 f.
  nature of, 14 f., 18, 24 f.
  private ownership of, 14
  sources of, 15
  as stored-up product of of labour, 17
Capital goods, demand for, 44, 101
Capitalism, contradictions of, 32, 48
  final crisis of, 48
  instability of, 54
Carlyle, Thomas, 22
Chamberlain, Joseph, 34, 37
Children's allowances, 87
Citizenship, industrial, 116
Class conflict, 33
Cobbett, William, 22
Collective bargaining, 33, 94, 107, 113, 149
Collectivism, 35, 37
Colonies, standard of living in, 122
Combination Acts, 28
Competition, 25, 26, 28, 54, 92

INDEX

Consultation, joint, 60, 107, 113, 117 f.
Consumer's choice, 62 f., 87 ff., 105, 110 f., 148, 150
   and economic planning, 88 ff.
   surplus, 81 f.
Consumption, 58 f.
   and investment, 64 ff.
   growth of, 32
Co-operative control of industry, 54
   farming, 119
   workshops, 119 f.
Corn Laws, 22
Costs, average and marginal, 93, 133
   comparative, 126 ff.
   decreasing and increasing, 91 ff.
   determination of, under Socialism, 90 ff., 147 f., 150
   international measurement of, 73 f., 129 f., 131 f., 132 ff.
   marginal, 133
   of social utilities, 109
Crises, economic, 42, 48
Cyclical fluctuations. *See* Trade Cycle.

DEMAND, anticipation of, 89, 91 f.
   collective, 109 ff.
   in relation to income structure, 88 ff.
   in relation to price, 10, 40
   public and private, 86 ff.
Democracy, economic, 55, 60, Chapter V *passim*.
   in United States, 115, 117
   nature of political, 60, 115, 116 f., 123
Depreciation and obsolescence, 64
De Tocqueville, A., 117
Development charges, 65
Dickinson, H. D., 145
Discrimination, 137 f.
Dismissals, 113
Dividends, limitation of, 69

ECONOMIC ACTIVITY, purpose of, 56 f.
   laws, nature of, 13, 26, 45, 105
   planning, errors in, 93 f.
   and public responsibility, 105
   international, 69 ff., 75 ff., 123 ff., 138 ff., Chapter VI *passim*. See also International Trade.
   national, 74, 75 f., Chapter IV *passim*, 130 ff., 140, 148 f.
Economics, growth of, 12 ff.
   of welfare, 77, 78

Socialist, difference from non-Socialist economics, 78 f.
    in relation to Economics in general, 10
    subject matter of, 8, 39
    static and dynamic theories of, 42
Economists, Austrian School, 41
    classical, 13 ff., 21 ff., 28, 31 ff., 38 f., 40 ff., 45, 80 ff., 143 ff.
    early Socialist, 20
Education, elementary, growth of, 33, 36
    technical, 28
Emigration, 19, 73, 126 f., 141
Employment, and socialisation. *See* Socialisation.
    Keynesian doctrine of, 43 ff.
    security of, 61
    State provision of, 37, 47, 48, 51 f.
Entrepreneurs, 15, 16, 18, 20 ff., 23 ff., 97, 131
Equality, economic, 30 ff., 33 f., 53, 57 f., 60, 66 ff., 79, 86, 105, 114, 147
    notion of, 29 f., 57
Equilibrium, classical theory of, 41 f., 43 ff., 46

FABIAN SOCIETY, 7, 34, 36, 37
Factors of production, prices of, 41 f., 83 f., 92 ff.
Factory Acts, 34, 107, 112
Food supply, 19
Foremen, choice of, 118
Franchise, extension of, 26, 116
Freedom of enterprise, 13 ff.
Free goods, supply of, 87 f.
Free Trade, 70, 72 f., 126, 128, 130
French Revolution, 12, 13, 29
Full employment, 37, 41 ff., 49 ff., 62 f., 98, 100, 121, 122, 140 f., 146, 149

GOLD STANDARD, 136

HEALTH SERVICES, public, 36, 62, 66, 88
Hobson, J. A., 43, 49
Hours, legal regulation of, 36, 39, 58
Housing, 62, 113

IMPERIALISM, 74
Import control, 71, 72 f.
Incentives, 11, 65 ff., 69, 103, 105, 106, 120 f., 147
    to private business, 102 f.
Incomes, distribution of, under Capitalism and Socialism, 65 ff., 68 ff., 84, 94 ff., 104 f., 122, 142, 149 f.

earned and unearned, 13, 52 f., 67 f., 84
professional, 52, 67
Socialist policy in relation to, 52 f.
Increasing misery theory, 32
Independent Labour Party, 37
Industrial Democracy, 54, 59 ff., Chapter V. *passim*.
and production, 119 ff.
Industrial Health Research Board, 113
Industrial Psychology, Institute of, 113
Industrial Revolution, 13, 14
Inequality, economic. *See under* Equality.
sentiment in favour of, 67 f.
Infant mortality, 19
Inflation, 46, 48
Inheritance, 13
Institutional revenue, 145
Interest, nature of, 22 ff., 100
rates of, 46, 50, 97 ff., 148
under socialisation, 100 f.
International trade, regulation of, 123 ff., 134 ff.
theory of, 40, 69 ff., 124 f., 126 ff.
International Working Men's Association, 37
Internationalism, 57, 58
Investment, 16, 21, 23, 27, 44 f., 48, 63 ff., 98

control of, 49, 51, 64, 79, 101, 102 f.
international, 76
public, 38, 46, 52, 64 f., 99 f.

JEVONS, W. S., 33, 35, 40
Journey to work, 114

KEYNES, Lord, 7, Chapter II *passim*, 77, 78, 97, 98

LABOUR, as commodity, 149, 150
compulsory, 59, 121
conditions of, 60
disutility of, 8, 56, 60, 107 f., 112
mobility of, 62, 111 f.
obligation to perform, 59
pleasure in, 56
Labour theory of value, 17, 40, 143
Laissez-faire, 9, 20, 45, 54, 70, 124
Land, agricultural value of, 104
as factor of production, 17
nationalisation of, 103
Landlords, claims of, 13, 14, 16, 22, 25
Lassalle, F., 37
Leisure, 8, 56, 58 f., 62, 106
Liquidity preference, 98

List, Friedrich, 128
Local Government, development of, 33, 116 f.
Location of industry, 50, 51 f.
Locke, John, 17

MALAYA, 73, 74, 122, 134 f.
Malthus, T. R., 19, 22, 32
Management, earnings of, 18
Marshall Aid, 137, 138 f.
Marshall, Alfred, 33, 35, 40, 41, 81
Marx, Karl, 30, 31, 32, 40, 142 ff.
Marxism, 35, 37, 40, 48, 142 ff.
Materialist Conception of History, 143
Measurability of economic factors, 7 f., 79, 107 ff., 118 f.
Menger, A., 40
Middle classes, rise of, 31
Mill, J. S., 31, 144
Minerals, 17
Monetary manipulation, 47
Money, control of supply, 69, 98
  in international trade, 123, 135 ff.
  marginal utility of, 82 f.
Monopoly, 13, 14, 18, 20, 22, 26, 47, 54, 74, 145, 146, 149

Morals in relation to Economics, 9
Multilateralism, 136. *See also* International Trade.

NATIONALISATION, 38, 53, 122. *See also* Socialisation.
Nationalism and economics, 74 f.
Needs. *See under* Wants.
New Towns, 52

OLD age pensions, 36. *See also* Pensions.
Owen, Robert, 20, 30, 37
Ownership, claims based on, 14, 15, 21 f., 22 ff., 25, 38, 83 f., 147

PEASANT producers and terms of trade, 74, 128 f.
Pensions, 67. *See also* Old age pensions.
Physiocrats, 13
Pigou, A. C., 77
Planning, economic, national. *See* Economic planning.
Poor Laws, 28, 36
Population, and land rent, 22
  Malthusian doctrine of, 18 f., 21, 32
Post Office, 54

Price policy in socialised industries, 102
  regulation, 52, 100
  system under Socialism, 81 ff., 89 ff.
Prices and costs, 90 ff., 147, 148
  agricultural, 131
  Marxian theory of, 144
Privilege, 20, 67, 83 f.
Production, maximum, as economic aim, 25 f., 59, 80 ff., 106 ff.
  measurement of, 84 ff.
Productivity, marginal, 42, 83 f.
Profit in relation to interest, 22 ff.
  margins, 100
Profit in public and private enterprise, 101 ff.
Progress, belief in, 27
Protectionism, 71, 128 f., 130 f., 133
Public Corporations. *See* Boards, Public.
Public works policy, 49, 50
Purchasing power, distribution of, 50, 80 ff.
  international, 135 f.

QUASI-RENT, 23
Quotas, 71, 126

RADICAL Programme, Unauthorised, 37

Rationalisation, 47
Rationing by prices, 146
Referendum, 115
Reform Act, 1867, 27, 33
  1884, 33
Rent, 22, 23, 25, 103 f., 148. *See also* Landlords.
Rent of ability, 24
Reserves, business, 65, 103
Ricardo, David, 25, 143, 145
Right to a trade, 26
  to work, 37
Rights of man, 9, 11 ff., 13, 21 f., 25, 29 f., 57, 62
  Declaration of, 57
Rights of property, 11 f., 13, 17, 20, 67
Risk-taking, 16, 24, 102
Rogers, Thorold, 34
Rousseau, J. J., 17
Rubber, 134

SAFETY precautions, 109
Salaries, 53
Savings, 14 f., 16, 18, 25, 99 f.
  and investment, 44 f. *See also* Investment.
Say, J. B., 24, 42
School meals, 36, 88
Security, economic, 61 f., 87 f.
Senior, Nassau, 24
Shaftesbury, Lord, 22
Shareholders, functions of, 20 f.
Shaw, Bernard, 68

Skill, acquisition of, 65 f.
Slave labour, 119
Smith, Adam, 13
Social Democratic Federation, 37
Social Insurance, 36, 87 f.
Socialisation, 53 ff., 64 f., 146. *See also* Nationalisation.
  and employment, 47, 99
Socialism, basis of, 9
  British, growth of, 34 ff., 38 f.
  evolutionary, 38, 143
  and internationalism, 74 ff., 122 ff.
  Keynes's view of, 47
  Utopian, 30
Soviet Union, 122
Specialisation, international, 70, 124, 127 f., 140
Speculation, 54, 132
Standard of living, minimum, 11, 12, 33, 34 f., 37, 38, 58 f., 61 f., 65 ff., 68, 79, 87 ff., 96 ff., 122 f.
  rising, 31, 32
State, as protector of property, 12
State control, limitations of, 49 ff.
  trading, 72, 137
Subsidies to consumption, 46, 90, 147
  to industry, 102
Supply and demand, laws of, 35 f.

TARIFFS, 70 f., 126, 137
Tax remissions, 46
Taxation, as a means of restricting consumption, 63, 89, 102, 147
  redistributive, 34, 36 f., 38, 39, 53, 87
Taylorism, 95
Town and country planning, 104, 113
Trade agreements, 71 f.
  bilateral, 133 f., 137 f.
Trade Cycle, 27, 42, 45, 64
Trade Unions, attitude of classical economists to, 26
  legal recognition of, 26 f., 33, 107, 113
  and production, 26
  and wages, 146, 149
Trading Estates, industrial, 52
Training for new jobs, 61

UNEMPLOYED, troubles (1880s), 37
Unemployment, in classical economic theory, 42
  inter-war, 43
  nature of, 27 f.
  Socialist views of, 47

Universal suffrage, 28, 30
Unpaid services, 63
Utilitarianism, 28, 29
Utility, 14, 56, 110
   marginal, 40
Utility goods, 52

VALUE, surplus, 146
   varying theories of, 40 f., 80 ff., 145 ff., 147 ff.
Varga, E., 48

WAGE differentials, 67, 95 ff., 112
Wages and costs in international trade, 73 f.
   and productivity, 33, 35
   fixing of, 94 f.
   in public services, 66 f.
   minimum, 36, 39
   nature of, 146
   policy, national, 68, 94 f., 148, 149 f.
   subsistence theory of, 18, 20, 21, 32 f., 35
Wages fund, theory, 19, 35
Walras, L., 40
Wants and needs, 57, 58, 59, 63, 82, 84, 86 ff.
   priority in supplying, 10 f., 57 f., 60, 62, 80 ff., 83, 84, 87 ff., 91
Webb, S. and B., 35
Welfare and economics, 77 ff., 150
   industrial, 109 f., 111 f.
Women workers and industrial democracy, 120
Workers' control. *See* Industrial Democracy.
Workshop control, 117 f.
World Government, 75